YAWN

YAWN

Adventures in Boredom

Mary Mann

FARRAR, STRAUS AND GIROUX

NEW YORK

Farrar, Straus and Giroux
18 West 18th Street, New York 10011

Library of Congress Cataloging-in-Publication Data
Names: Mann, Mary.
Title: Yawn : adventures in boredom / Mary Mann.
Other titles: Adventures in boredom
Description: First edition. | New York : FSG Originals, 2017.
Identifiers: LCCN 2016041343 | ISBN 9780374535841 (paperback) |
    ISBN 9780374714420 (e-book)
Subjects: LCSH: Boredom. | Boredom—History. | Boredom—Social
    aspects. | Meaning (Psychology) | BISAC: SOCIAL SCIENCE /
    Popular Culture.
Classification: LCC BF575.B67 M36 2017 | DDC 152.4—dc23
LC record available at https://lccn.loc.gov/2016041343

Designed by Jo Anne Metsch

Our books may be purchased in bulk for promotional, educational,
or business use. Please contact your local bookseller or the
Macmillan Corporate and Premium Sales Department at
1-800-221-7945, extension 5442, or by e-mail at
MacmillanSpecialMarkets@macmillan.com.

www.fsgbooks.com • www.fsgoriginals.com
www.twitter.com/fsgbooks • www.facebook.com/fsgbooks

1 3 5 7 9 10 8 6 4 2

To my family, and to Grant

CONTENTS

YAWN

IN A CUBICLE WITH
THE DESERT FATHERS

We were talking about work, naturally. The table was littered with beer bottles and the view out the plate-glass restaurant window was of a street in Kansas City, but it could have been a street in any number of towns. Our conversation was as typical as our surroundings, down to Nate summing up his job in the pharmaceutical industry with "Yeah, I'm bored at work all the time."

There are few more ordinary sentiments. Over 70 percent of Americans, and 80 percent of people worldwide, are bored with or actively dislike their jobs. None of us sitting around the table that night knew this statistic, but we did know plenty of people, which amounted to more or less the same thing. Nate said he could "count on one hand the people I know who bounce out of bed excited to go to work."

One of them was his wife, Amy, sitting next to him in a crisp, white collared shirt even though it was a Saturday (Nate wore a faded Royals T-shirt). Amy had decided she wanted to be a lawyer when she was twelve and never wavered, even during her Alice Cooper years—which was how we'd met, because her skull-and-crossbones T-shirt and my patchwork corduroys were the only non-pantsuits at a Women in Leadership seminar we both attended in college. Amy no longer dyes her hair black but she's still on the same path, still corresponds with the seminar speakers; less than a decade after the seminar, she *is* a woman in leadership, with an in-house counsel gig at a global bank. Meanwhile, I'd burned through more careers than Nate, which, he agreed, was saying something.

It worried me, this restlessness, so much so that I'd begun studying boredom itself in hopes of finding answers. I didn't know until that night in Kansas City that Nate was similarly concerned, and that he'd also been talking and thinking quite a bit about boredom as a result. "Most people are relieved when I bring it up," he told me. "Like, *Oh, thank god, someone I can talk to about this.* So now I'm more comfortable with talking about boredom than I used to be, and that helps a lot. Because, you know, boredom doesn't mean it's not a good job. I'm busy. I make a living. I just don't know if I'll ever be *that* into work. Which feels weird to say." Amy scooted closer to him, and he put his arm around her and smiled at his driven wife, with whom he raises chickens and dogs, plays video games, and attends Royals games. "But I have other things

I *do* care about," he added. "At the end of the day, I have to ask: What's really so shitty about being bored at work?"

The question nagged me all the way back to New York, back to the fifth-floor walk-up where I live with my boy-friend, our fingers perpetually crossed in hopes that our landlord won't raise the rent. *What's really so shitty about being bored at work?* It takes two jobs to cover my portion of rent: working as a writing associate at a college and as a researcher for private clients, which is kind of like being a private detective, without the danger and sex. Most of my work is done in libraries—from the dim stacks of Co-lumbia to the tourist-crammed halls of Schwarzman, with its grand columns and stone lions—though sometimes I also conduct interviews. Once I interviewed a *real* private detective, a former city cop who'd quit the force, moved to New Jersey, and found detective work a nice change of pace. He explained how he tails people on the subway ("you never get in the same car as your mark; it's too ob-vious") and described a stakeout: sitting awake and alert in his car throughout the night, no radio, no book or TV, resisting the urge to look at his phone because "if you miss that moment"—usually the moment the adulterer leaves the hotel—"you don't get paid."

I envied his single-minded focus. We both enjoyed our work, the detective and I, and both felt lucky to be doing what we were doing, but for some reason I was still restless, easily distracted, checking my phone or the

fridge or jolting back into work mode after finding myself knee-deep in a daydream, even while working under
multiple tight deadlines. It bothered me, this restlessness;
made me wonder if something was wrong with me. But
Nate had a similar experience, and so, I was finding, did
many other people. The more I asked around, the more
common this restlessness seemed to be. Even friends who
always complained about job stress and heavy workloads
confessed to checking Facebook multiple times a day, or
keeping up running conversations on Slack or Gchat. It
seemed that nobody was always fully engaged in what
they were doing, a trend I'd assumed was obviously bad,
a sign of something flawed in our generation or our culture or our moment in time, until Nate's question, *What's
really so shitty about being bored at work?*

Maybe nothing. As the light shining through the
apartment window began to fade, I studied the growing
piles of books referencing boredom, from academic studies to novels, that had come to dominate the living room
as I embarked on a self-assigned study of the enemy, like
Sherlock's obsession with Moriarty (though again, less
dangerous). I picked them up, put them down again,
looked out the window at the clouds, which scudded
across the pinkening sky in a way that called to mind
the easily forgotten fact that New York is a seaside town,
which in turn reminded me of Melville and the "insular
city of the Manhattoes, belted round by wharves as In-
dian isles by coral reefs." My mom used to paint pictures
of the sea, and the sunset was always the first thing on
her list of reasons why not to be bored. "How can you be

bored in a world with sunsets?" she'd ask, a trace of desperation in her voice, a hint of *Oh, man, you kids have no idea, and anyway, aren't* you *supposed to be the ones reawakening* our *sense of childlike wonder?* Boredom when we were kids was a problem to be solved, with craft projects or books or playing with our friends or TV if nothing else. It was worrying to find that these solutions just amounted to procrastination in the working world, where being busy didn't necessarily mean not being bored, not by a long shot. Friends my age were all a little bit worn-out and weary and slightly shocked, still, nearly ten years after college, by the realization that this was it: these offices were where we would spend most of our waking lives. But few people (Nate excepted) seemed to want to talk about it at length, and there were never any real solutions presented for adults, besides *Be grateful for what you have* and *Only boring people get bored*, which didn't scrub away the feeling, just coated it in a fine sheen of self-reproach. Nate's attitude seemed more reasonable: boredom wasn't the problem-to-be-squelched I'd grown up thinking it was—it was normal. Which maybe meant it wasn't worth thinking about so much. I could ditch the books and stop worrying about why things are the way they are.

A phone conversation with my cousin Connie only strengthened these misgivings. Connie works in an orange juice concentrate factory, an experience I'd imagined as like that of the former autoworker Ben Hamper, who wrote in his memoir *Rivethead*: "Car, windshield. Car, windshield. Drudgery piled atop drudgery. Cigarette to cigarette. Decades rolling through the rafters, bones turning to dust, stubborn clocks gagging down flesh, another wind-shield, another cigarette . . ." (except juice instead of cars, and no cigarettes, since food-producing factories have to be more hygienic). I expected boredom, and I expected complaining. All seemed promising at first: when I asked if her job was interesting, Connie chuckled and answered, "Not really." But when I asked if she liked it, it was as if she'd never even considered the question. "Do I *like* it?" she repeated. There was a moment of silence on her end. "Well, it's regular work. And I don't have to deal with people. I wish they'd let us have music, but nobody minds if I sing. And I have a lot of time to think and plan things. Yeah, honey, it's a fine job. Why, are you looking for one?"

"No. Thanks, though," I replied, glancing at the books piled on the ottoman, spilling onto the floor, which I noticed could use a cleaning. I had plenty of work. I was looking for answers.

Through the books on the ottoman I'd learned that workplace boredom hasn't been around that long, at least not the way it's understood today. In the preindustrial era "sons simply did the jobs (or, higher up the hierarchy, moved into the positions) that their fathers picked for them," according to the historian Thomas Lutz. There would have been no point in labeling a job *boring* or *interesting*, because there weren't any alternatives. So useless would these words have been that they didn't exist in English until the 1800s, after the Industrial Revolution created loads of new jobs and thus introduced the workforce to the novel idea of options.

Now we have the language to make comparisons between boring and interesting work, plus an unprecedented ability to compare. The Internet and mass media shape our worldview to such a degree that the ethnographer Martin Demant Frederiksen—who's studied boredom and depression among young men in the Republic of Georgia—told me he couldn't imagine what his study would have looked like without them. "The Internet especially had a massive impact in terms of the men realizing how marginal Georgia is in relationship to the world," he explained. "It made it much more obvious to them how boring a city they lived in."

When my sister and I complained about how boring the town we grew up in was, tucked away as it was in industrial northern Indiana, our mom, a nurse, would say that comparisons were odious, and our dad, a preacher, would remind us that covetousness was a sin. Do not covet thy neighbor's Disney vacation, for example, or thy neighbor's Barbie car. As an adult, try not to covet thy neighbor's globe-trotting job or thy neighbor's seeming sense of abiding purpose. Our parents were just being parents, giving advice they hoped would shape us into functional expectation-managing adults. But over the years I've wanted, and watched *them* want, enough things to wonder if wanting *not* to covet things was just another want, another not-good-enough pang, like coveting Connie's sense of chill or Nate's ability to manage his expectations or a seventeenth-century farmhand's vocabulary, lacking the word for boredom along with any notion of its being shitty or not.

I can't be someone else, or live in a different era. What I *can* do is research. With a deep sigh (what my mom—whose own restlessness has led her to explore many alternatives to nursing over the years, including Reiki certification—calls a cleansing breath) I scooped up the books on the floor, straightened them up in two neat stacks on the ottoman, picked an unread one, and settled back on the couch so the lamplight hit the pages.

Long before there was an English word for boredom, a group of men began their workday in silence, a complete and all-encompassing silence, unbroken by traffic or birdsong. Their offices were insulated by miles and miles of sand, valleys and hills and rivers of sand, the uniformity broken here and there by a pile of sand-colored rocks. Singing birds and lowing cattle and barking dogs couldn't live there. Most humans wouldn't attempt it either, which was exactly why these men had set up shop in Egypt's Nitrian Desert. They were the Desert Fathers, and their job was communing with God.

In some ways their surroundings weren't so different from those of a modern corporation. Free from nature noises, the Desert Fathers still had one another's sounds to contend with, pacing and sniffling, throat-clearing and muttering, turning pages, gulping water—repetitive human sounds like those you might obsess over in an equally subdued office, the tick-tick-tick of typing or a coworker's habitual phone-answering cadence. Many of the Desert Fathers also worked in cubicles, more or less, living and praying in tiny side-by-side cells. Other times they shared cells, kneeling in the sand in a dystopian version of the open-plan office.

This particular impression of the Fathers—who are more often remembered as wild-eyed mystics than as proto–office workers—comes from the writings of a fourth-century monk named Cassian, who lived with and observed the Desert Fathers in hopes of creating a similar setup in France. Their biggest challenge was an invisible enemy, Cassian explained, "which we may describe as tedium or perturbation of heart," attacking around noon and inducing "such lassitude of body and craving for food, as one might feel after . . . hard toil . . . Finally one gazes anxiously here and there, and sighs that no brother of any description is to be seen approaching: one is forever in and out of one's cell, gazing at the sun as though it were tarrying to its setting."

Elsewhere in the same essay, he wrote in a more personal tone, "Towards any work that may be done within the enclosure of our own lair, we become listless and inert."

While reading Cassian's words I imagined the characters from the American version of *The Office*, their desks morphed into cells, the omnipresent clock replaced with the slow-setting sun. I pictured a monk Jim faking a swoon as a visiting nun named Pam explained in a voice-over: "Every so often, Jim dies of boredom." Maybe the Fathers' plight was funnier than they knew, I thought, imagining a Michael Scott monk running from cell to cell, robes flying behind him as he rushed to share bad puns with his fellow monks, all to avoid the small amount of work waiting in his own cell. Maybe their invisible enemy really wasn't *so* bad.

Similar logic informed my friend Sonya's therapist's suggestion that she cope with her ultra-boring corporate job by visualizing herself in an episode of *The Office*. "It's supposed to help me be less annoyed by making me feel like a passive observer," Sonya told me when we met for happy hour on a rainy evening. "I'm supposed to laugh at stuff, let it slide off, instead of thinking, *Oh god, this is my life*." She'd put a recurring reminder on her calendar, so the words "The Office" appeared on her phone every morning at ten o'clock, but eventually removed it because "it started to feel like second nature."

It helped, she said, but didn't entirely fix things. She was able to laugh at the tediousness and seeming pointlessness of her office, where every project dragged on indefinitely, her work going unread and ignored, everyone around her reading Twitter or the news or watching YouTube videos with headphones on. But she still found the basic acts of waking up, going to work, and making it through the day to feel more daunting than they should have—"It's just work, not war." She might have simply quit, saved some time and annoyance and therapy hours, if it wasn't for the money.

I wonder what percentage of the boredom people put up with is endured for money. It's high, judging by how closely the emotion is associated with work (and school, preparing us for work). If he didn't need money, I'm certain Nate wouldn't work at all—nearly every other facet of his life gives him more sense of purpose than his job.

Even Connie would "love to be retired," but doesn't get paid enough to stop working anytime soon.

Sonya has the opposite problem. She's being paid heaps, and will get a bonus on top of that on her one-year anniversary. All she has to do is . . . nothing. "I come in at ten," she told me, "and I finish all my work by like ten-seventeen. I used to try to supplement that with self-initiated projects, but that just made people angry. Now I watch the clock, or do something non-work-related and feel guilty. So. Just two hundred and forty-seven more days of that." She didn't hesitate in calculating the days; like a cartoon prisoner making hash marks on a cell wall, she's been keeping close track.

"I mean, what the fuck," she added. "If I have any perspective at all: it's a year, I do nothing, I make money. How is that so hard?" *What's really so shitty about being bored at work?* Coming straight from the office, Sonya was able to answer her own question immediately: "It *feels* hard. It's your time, and it's being wasted. It hurts your soul and your mind and your brain. It's a shitty feeling, especially when you know you're capable of being useful."

When we met seven years ago, Sonya was one of those people who thrived on work. She was the product manager of a tech start-up, and she was constantly needed: answering questions, putting out fires, building and refining strategies to make everything run smoother. A mutual friend once caught sight of Sonya leaving a lunch meeting and described her as "like the president in *The West Wing*": striding down the street, surrounded by a scrum of coworkers asking urgent questions that she answered decisively. She was *necessary* for the building of a brand-new company, and the confidence that gave her spilled over into the rest of her life. When the start-up was folded into the corporation she works for now, she knew things would be different, but she didn't know how much that would change her. Now, she says, she doubts what she's good at—"Losing that sense of yourself doesn't take long"—and the malaise of the new office has seeped into her life. "I'm exhausted all the time, more than I ever used to be after a day of back-to-back meetings," she told me. "I'm always just *straining* toward the end of the day."

It was something a Desert Father might have said in confession, except . . . Sonya's eyes were narrowed with anger about her wasted time and her own choice to stay, and I pictured the Desert Father's eyes filled with tears. In my mind the Father looked like my own father, an association not solely based on their identical titles; my dad has always woken up to pray before the sun rises, a ritual of bringing himself closer to God that he's had since before he became a priest, but by nightfall he's inevitably earthbound like the rest of us, so exhausted by disenchantment that he barely has the energy to drink a beer in front of a *M*A*S*H* rerun. I used to think he was just another guy who didn't like his job, like Willy Loman in *Death of a Salesman* or Peter Gibbons in *Office Space*. But now I also have work I wake up voluntarily early for, and I understand that weariness or restlessness experienced while doing something you care about feels different from being bored at any old job. It feels a lot like failing.

For the Desert Fathers, monkhood wasn't just a career; it was a calling—the thing they were born to do, the reason for their very existence. This idea of a calling began in the religious world and spread to the secular as more and more people began to have career choices. If you have more than one option, how do you know which job to pursue? Well, which one *calls* to you? "Following a calling" lends a pleasing mystical flavor to job selection, and suggests that whatever moneymaking endeavor we spend most of our waking hours doing might also be spiritually fulfilling. It also soothes anxieties over our limited life spans: if we're following a calling then we're spending our time well, using it for something we care about rather than losing it to pointless work.

Over the last decade, the phrase "Do what you love" has appeared on posters and T-shirts and social media. It's become so prominent that it has provoked backlash against the slogan, which seems to snub anyone who can't afford a degree and the time to figure out what they love. Many people now understand it as a classist notion. Yet the idea behind it persists, having been deeply engrained in our culture long before Instagram images of posters in tech offices. "Our work must be the chief natural interest in life," wrote the Jesuit scholar John C. Kelly in 1949. "If our life does not pivot round our work, we can never be at equilibrium."

It's an unbelievable amount of pressure to put on one thing. A period of disinterest, even just an hour, might send the whole thing toppling. How can you claim to love something that has the potential to bore you? How can you make any claim on it at all? Plagued with boredom, the Desert Fathers were also wracked with guilt for feeling bored and doubtful about their calling, which had heretofore been the very reason for their existence. This compound of bad feelings was known as "the 'demon of noontide,'" according to the theologian Michael Raposa, "a powerful boredom that 'besieges' the devotee, resulting in distraction from, sometimes even abandonment of, the spiritual life."

In this light Sonya seemed almost lucky, in the same off-kilter way that Romeo and Juliet were lucky—she'd loved and lost and never risked the possibility that decades of routine might chip away at that certainty. Meanwhile, I still feel lucky to be doing the work I do, talking with students and playing private detective in the library stacks, but every stray moment of boredom feels like a small betrayal I've committed against luck, and a frightening reminder that I might not feel so lucky forever. If Sonya were a character in a book or play I might feel a perverse envy for her, similarly to how people experience *Romeo and Juliet* as a great love story. But she wasn't a character, she was my friend, and it broke my heart to see my strong friend look at me with fear in her eyes and say, "Honestly, Mary, these past few months are the closest I've ever been to depression."

After a few more drinks and a couple of tacos, we said our goodbyes and good lucks and, hoping to cheer up, I walked home, splashing defiantly through rain puddles in my galoshes and observing other happy hours in other bars. In one window, three slim men in blazers leaned against a counter, bodies canted toward one another, and sipped from squat glasses with visible relief. In a window farther south, bar tables looked like dollhouse furniture next to five huge guys with unidentifiable insignias on their shirts—firemen or a bowling league, or maybe the military. I forded another puddle and recalled having read that happy hour originated in the military, in the navy specifically, as a period of entertainment for sailors whose lives were otherwise full of routine tasks and unvarying seascapes, "exceedingly monotonous and forbidding," as Melville's Ishmael put it, "not the slightest variety that I could see."

It used to seem like such nonsense that Ishmael could describe the sea like that and still want to work on a boat. He didn't just want to; he *needed* to—it was the only cure he knew for feeling "grim about the mouth," so dull and irritable that he longed to run into the street and start knocking strangers' hats off. This inconsistency always bugged me, not least because it was the basis for everything else in *Moby-Dick*, including long meditations on ship rope. These encyclopedia-like passages are strangely pleasurable to read, but they also add to the impression that ship life really is *that* dull—not at all worth getting mixed up with Ahab for.

I began to change my mind after meeting Lindsay. It was the semester after the Women in Leadership seminar, which hadn't managed to take—I was feeling no stirrings toward law, business, or politics—and we were both assisting a biologist named Gail who once told us flat-out that she preferred primates to people. Gail wasn't much for conversation, so Lindsay and I were often left to our own devices, and we got to know each other well. She was from Alaska and had worked in the salmon industry ever since she got her first job in a cannery at sixteen. The summer before we met had been her first on a fishing boat: at sea for weeks at a time, tracking down schools of salmon, dropping nets and hauling the fishes' flopping forms up and into the waiting hold. I recognized that this meant performing the same set of tasks over and over again and not seeing anyone, besides her crewmates, for weeks at a time. Still, as she described her summer framed in sparkle and spray, it appeared startlingly 3-D next to my own July and August spent tossing pizzas and sweeping up pepperoni spills in the walk-in. When she e-mailed me with an application for a guiding job at a friend's kayak company, I knocked my roommate's printer off the shelf in my hurry to submit it. "Almost all men in their degree," said Ishmael in his knocking-off-hats phase, "some time or other, cherish very nearly the same feelings towards the ocean with me."

My Alaska story has no sparkle and spray; it's mostly gray—pale gray sky, medium gray rain, dark gray sea. I paddled my kayak slowly, so as to keep pace with the tourists, pointing out eagles' nests and rattling off Alaska facts during each of the four two-hour tours I led every day. It was more routine than any job I've had since. The only speck of sparkle was Lindsay, driving the motorboat that shuttled tourists to and from the tours, her red cheeks a beacon as she grinned into the rain-flecked wind. At the end of the day I'd watch her tie up the boat, pull up the motor, do all the countless little things she did every single other day at this time. It was all very relaxing to watch because of the way she did it, so clearly satisfied by the repetitive physicality of the work, like a basketball player practicing free throws or a singer doing vocal exercises.

This is what the psychologist Mihaly Csikszentmihalyi calls "flow": being so single-mindedly absorbed in what you're doing that you may lose track of time. It's the optimal state of human experience, according to Csikszentmihalyi. "The purpose of the flow is to keep on flowing, not looking for a peak or utopia but staying in the flow." Flow is most commonly associated with people whose jobs are physically or creatively demanding—athletes, artists, musicians, scientists—though I did speak to an accountant who told me he experiences something like flow during tax season. He told me this with a delight that suggested there might be something extra special about experiencing flow while performing a dry and repetitive activity, something that would just frustrate almost anyone else. We expect to be delighted by variety, hence commercials always touting products as "new and improved." It's a pleasant surprise to be delighted by sameness.

Several years after we worked together, I called Lindsay to ask her a question I was always too embarrassed to bring up when I lived in Alaska: Was she ever bored at work? "No," she said, "not really." Fishing is tedious, she said—the work is repetitive, the view monotonous, the crew unchanging—but she'd just finished her seventh season and rarely *felt* bored. Which is not to say she's incapable of boredom. A couple of years ago she briefly held a job as a full-time newspaper reporter. "I started in September," she told me, "then it got to be April and I got restless, then it got to be May and I was like, *oh my god, why am I in this office every day*." By June she couldn't take it anymore—she went part-time at the paper so she could run a water taxi for half the week. "That first day I was soaring. I couldn't believe how much better I felt on a boat."

Just that hint of splash and sparkle, and Ishmael's desire to "get to sea as soon as I can" surged within me. But the feeling quickly passed, ushered out by the memory of performing my end-of-day guiding routines—sliding kayaks up onto racks, stacking paddles, sorting damp life jackets by size, all the while thinking: *I would so much rather be reading about this.*

It was lucky, then, that I ended up in libraries, spending all the hours that I'm not working with students instead on fact-finding missions for clients, searching for seventeenth-century town records or twentieth-century free speech violations or whatever else I'm fishing for that day. Fresh air and sun aside, the stacks do have their similarities to the sea—row after row of books like wave after wave of water, the smell of old paper as distinctive and pervasive as that of salt.

Submerged in this dim and dusty deep one morning, I sat cross-legged on the floor between two shelves of 802s (literature, miscellany) and trawled for phrases from a thick red book. *It's the surprise of this enforced idleness. It makes you feel not at home with yourself.* That was Nora Watson, editor. *I don't think it's terribly different from somebody who works on the assembly line forty hours a week and comes home cut off, numb, dehumanized.* Roberta Victor, prostitute. *You got to keep from going crazy from boredom.* Frank Decker, truck driver. "It is about a search," wrote Studs Terkel in the introduction to *Working*, his book of interviews with people about their jobs, "for daily meaning as well as daily bread. For a sort of life rather than a Monday through Friday sort of dying."

Terkel's book was published in 1974, and more than four decades later I was having conversations with people about the same damn thing—about the 80 percent of people worldwide who are unhappy at work and the 20 percent who are happy, often in jobs that might bore anyone else into a stupor. There was no clear solution, no obvious path away from restlessness and into the clear light of flow. The unsolvable nature of the project I'd given myself was making me itchy. If I were a detective I would have opened my desk drawer and pulled out a bottle of whiskey and two glasses, one for me and one for my suspicious but strangely compelling new client. If I were a ship's captain I would have pulled a flask from my boot and taken a deep drink as I stared at the horizon, muttering that I'd get my deep-dwelling nemesis if it was the last thing I did. But I'm a researcher, and outside beverages aren't allowed in the library, so I stood, stretched my legs, and walked away from the 802s. I had other work to do—searching for pieces of information that it would not be my job to make sense of, and earning an hourly rate in the process.

Dust motes floated around me, library plankton, as I made my way to the 550s, or earth sciences. I'd come to the library that day at the behest of an artist who was doing a project involving ice. The exact parameters of the project were unclear to me—possibly she was making something out of ice, or doing a concept piece about ice, or maybe ice was just a side component of a larger project—but for my purposes none of that mattered. I was hired for ice facts, and ice facts I would obtain.

Through the stacks and down the stairwell I went, alone. As a freelancer, I'm usually alone while I work, and for the most part I like it that way. No coworkers whose habits impose even more of a sense of routine on my everyday, like a co-copywriter at my last job who got up to get candy from the receptionist's desk at ten o'clock on the dot every morning (and who was probably equally irked by my own candy bowl visits at four every afternoon), or, at the upscale yoga clothing store where I worked before that, a fellow saleswoman who approached each customer with an identically cadenced *"Hi* there! What are *you* looking for today?" No boss with complete salary-based control of my time. My time is my own and the cast of people who fill it is constantly changing. On a bad day, this means every wasted hour is my own fault, not to mention unpaid, and there's nobody around who can sympathize.

Well, the latter isn't strictly true. About one in three working Americans is an independent worker, according to the Freelancers Union, and at any given moment, I can go online and find many of these fifty-four million people tweeting or blogging or otherwise sharing with the world what it's like to work alone and have control of their own time. They wake up early and go to coworking spaces or they treat themselves to matinees and work late into the night; they post pictures of window-facing desks or dogs napping at their feet or the coffee shops they frequent, full of other freelancers fighting over outlets and nursing six-dollar lattes. I used to turn to this online community when I was having an off day, but it only ever made me feel worse—more physically alone, and more useless with time management, the could-have-been work hours sliding by as I idly scrolled entries for a contest over who on Twitter could come up with the most disturbing twist on a children's book title. Our time was ours; were we so afraid of boredom or loneliness or the combination of the two that this was how we wanted to spend it? My own contest entry, *No Margaret, God Isn't There. He Never Was*, was mostly disturbing in that it betrayed my fear that there was no overarching purpose for my time. I canceled my Twitter account soon afterward, and not long after that began reading about boredom during those restless moments instead. I began e-mailing experts to set up interviews in person or over Skype. On days like that one spent searching for ice facts in the library, I found books that dealt with boredom and stopped the clock for my client while I jotted down notes for what was rapidly becoming a project. I liked the sound of that, "project"—like a bucket for my time to pour into, so that not a drop of it was wasted. Exploring other people's restlessness lent some purpose to my own.

With this on my mind I was easily waylaid in the 658s (management, general management) by a book called *Selling with Noble Purpose*. The author, the management consultant Lisa Earle McLeod, found that the highest-earning salespeople were those who truly believed that their products helped customers. They were also happier. These people weren't confined to one type of product or line of work; they could be found everywhere from pharmaceutical companies, like the one that employs Nate, to political campaigns. According to a congressional staffer friend of McLeod's, there's a "true believer" in every office, "that starry-eyed optimist who still believes they can make a difference. But here's the thing all the jaded staffers don't tell you—everyone else in the office is secretly jealous of the true believer." Thus the mission of McLeod's book is to give the "secret true believer inside of us . . . permission to come out."

It might have been tempting if I wasn't only a few years out of a job that *did* give me that permission, a sales position at that yoga clothing store where my coworker greeted each customer in the same cadence. Really, the permission we were given to unleash our "secret true believer" was more like an ultimatum—even if we didn't completely buy the premise that selling expensive yoga clothes was meaningful work, we were expected to at least *act* like we believed. From the outside the company's insistence on retail as a mission seemed nice, the kind of validation that salespeople rarely get, but once inside I quickly learned that a sense of purpose isn't something you can just will into existence. The store's enforced optimism just exaggerated my tendencies toward doubt and cantankerousness until I felt like a cartoon version of my worst self: that unstable bar patron who gives teary-eyed lectures to anyone who'll listen about the inevitable self-inflicted doom of humanity. *Capitalism!* I'd proclaim over my fourth beer when I ran out of cogent arguments, as if the word itself said everything there was to say about days and weeks and months spent selling products nobody really needs to people who already have enough of said products anyway.

It was a bad time, a weird time, an embarrassing time, and I was jealous of anyone who had a job that seemed to have *real* purpose, like my friend Erica in nonprofit marketing. But when I asked her, she told me the world of social enterprise and nonprofits is also more complicated than it might appear to an outsider. "Your company can have a purpose, but that doesn't mean you do," she explained. "It's not transitive." Around the same time, Sonya was worrying that she wouldn't like her new job at a tech start-up because it didn't have a cause, per se—it wasn't trying to cure poverty or clothe the kids of Africa or make people care about opera again. But she was surprised and grateful to see herself become one of those people whom Nate had declared to be so rare, who "bounce out of bed

excited to go to work." It was less about being a true believer, per se, and more about feeling useful; in her current role at the big corporation she registers the absence
of this usefulness as boredom.

Some researchers argue that this is boredom's function, or at least one of them. "Boredom is an emotional
signal that makes people very aware that in their current
situation there is a lack of purpose," the social psychologist
Wijnand van Tilburg told me. Before we spoke, I'd read
several studies of Van Tilburg's to this effect, and put them
in a folder along with an essay by the psychoanalyst Adam
Phillips that declares: "Boredom is integral to the process
of taking one's time." Even with an alert system, it still
takes patience—trying and failing and trying again—for
an individual to figure out which activities give him or
her a sense of purpose. There's no tried-and-true company
or position or lifestyle that works for everyone.

If the Desert Fathers are any indication, the need for
patience doesn't ever truly go away, even once you find a
purpose. The work that they were willing to give up everything and move to the middle of nowhere for, the work
that brought them the greatest joy, also sometimes bored
them to tears. "It sounds a lot like parenthood," joked our
downstairs neighbor, a fellow freelancer as well as a
mother of two, when I mentioned the Fathers to her—
a comment that shed a different light on my instinctual
comparison of the Fathers to my dad, as well as on my
mom's standard plea for us to stop saying we were bored
and start appreciating the sunset instead. "This is where
you're going to judge me," said our neighbor when I asked

to know more; then she launched into the many tedious aspects of parenting, from figuring out how to plan the kids' summers so they're not overscheduled but don't just "stare at me all day," to repetitive readings of the same favored books, to waiting, waiting, waiting for the kids to do such basic things as figure out what they want to wear and how to put it on. "Why would you think I'd judge you for that?" I asked afterward. "Well, I love my kids," she answered, "and you're not supposed to be bored with people you love."

I understood what she was saying; it was similar to the monks' feeling guilty when they were bored in their cells, or my feeling like a failure when I grow restless while researching. If boredom is an alert system that tells us what we're doing lacks purpose, in a roundabout way it might imply that her kids don't matter to her, though they clearly do. And research matters to me, even though, lost in thought, I'd overshot the 550s and ended up all the way down in the 095s (books notable for their bindings) in the sub-sub-basement of the library, almost as rarely visited by humans as the deepest parts of the sea. I felt for the dust-layered books—it's hard going it alone—and took a few minutes to admire their celebrated bindings before turning around and heading back up the stairs, bound for ice facts, back to work.

2

SPICING IT UP

We were early. I peered through the glass door and saw only a handful of disparate shoppers and two saleswomen, one leaning against the wall behind the counter, swiping her thumb over an iPhone screen, while the other fidgeted, paced, adjusted merchandise, and surveyed the store, looking this way and that, until her eyes locked on mine through the door.

"Doesn't look like it's happening," I said, hurriedly turning away. "Well, that's okay—I know you weren't too psyched on it anyway. Let's just get a drink."

"Wait, that lady's coming this way, I bet she knows. Hold on." And with that, Grant—ever practical, ever diligent—opened the door and stepped through. "Excuse me, miss?" I heard him say. "Is this the right place for the sexy trivia event? My girlfriend found it online, but we weren't sure . . ." And then he was waving me in. And then I was opening the door. And then, before you could say *Sex and the City,* I was standing in front of a wall of dildos in all the colors of the rainbow, plastic glass of sparkling wine in hand, listening to a saleswoman pitch my boyfriend on the benefits of double penetration.

We were there because I'd googled the phrase "spice things up"—a term I'd seen and heard plenty of times, the stuff of sitcom conversations and advice columns and listicles on life-improvement blogs. Gotten into the habit of eating dinner while watching your shows together every night? Spice things up. Leaning on the same go-to sex positions every time? Spice things up. Do your kisses look less like movie makeouts and more like pecks from your grandmother with every passing day? Spice things up, and fast.

It was one of those phrases, ubiquitous and vague, that I hadn't given much thought to before scanning the library archives for boredom and coming across study after study about sex, from "Was Bob Seger Right? Relation Between Boredom in Leisure and [Risky] Sex" to "The Relationship Between Boredom Proneness and Solitary Sexual Behaviors in Adults"—all more or less equally disheartening. Sex is one of the few aspects of boredom on which researchers tend to agree; unluckily for Grant and me, entering our fourth year of dating and our second of living together, what they agree on is that monogamous sex gets boring. "Boredom and accumulated resentments," write John Watt and Jackie Ewing in *The Journal of Sex Research,* "are the greatest obstacles to continued growth

of a sexual relationship." Unlike the blithe can-do attitude of the listicle, these studies excavated the human
psyche, carefully identified and extricated a seminal problem, dusted it off, dropped it on the reader, and just left it
there, unsolved and stinking. The closest thing to advice
in the piles of studies was a conclusion reached by the psychologists Aneta Tunariu and Paula Reavey in *Sexual and
Relationship Therapy*: "Novelty, mystery and uncertainty,
alongside physical and psychological distance, danger,
conflict and hostility, instigate and facilitate sexual passion
for both men and women"—an unhealthy-sounding list
of ways to spice things up.

There was no way to read these studies and not think
about my own relationship, which, though neither in a rut
nor rife with excitement-seeking conflict, was statistically
bound for one or the other eventually, and I was deep into
the phase of research where statistics seem like everything. I'd spent days reading the findings of experts who
dedicated years of their lives to culling the experiences
and feelings of thousands of people, who in turn gave
hours of *their* lives to the experts in question. What was
the purpose of all this time expended if I didn't take their
findings seriously? Someday down the road one or the
other of us would grow bored of our sex life, and the experts had no real tips for weathering this impending storm.
So I did what any other solution-oriented person who
came of age in the twenty-first century might do, and got
ahead of the game by googling "spice things up."

Solutions came fast and thick, which is not meant to
be a dick joke, but everything starts to come out like one

when you've been googling information even tangentially related to sex. If you understood humanity solely through the Internet you'd think that sex, not work, was how we spent most of our time. There are hundreds of thousands of sex toys to buy, an uncountable number of pornos to watch, and more lists of advice than I could read in a lifetime, including "9 Tips for Steamy Shower Sex," "67 New Blow-His-Mind Moves," "8 Sex Tips Inspired by Shakira," and "14 Car Sex Tips That Won't Get You Injured or Arrested."

An hour in, I was more overwhelmed than turned on. My search had been too broad; we don't even have a car. But we do live in New York, and what the city lacks in opportunities for road head it makes up for in events. A search for "sex spice New York event" yielded tantric yoga workshops, sacred yoni seminars, sexologist lectures, and even an all-inclusive pirate-themed "fantasy vacation" with aphrodisiac snacks and private hours in a dungeon. Then, finally, there was something that seemed a little more reasonable: a free public event at a reputable sex-positive sex-toy store called "Sexy Trivia and Cocktail Party"—"Add some spice (and cocktails) to your Friday night," the description read. I e-mailed the event link to Grant with "Research trip" as the subject line. *Will you come with me?* I typed above the link. *I promise we'll leave if it gets weird. Also, free drinks!*

"Wanna buy something?" whispered Grant after we'd been sipping champagne for fifteen minutes. Trivia was coming, the saleswoman had assured us. We just weren't sure when. "I feel bad standing around this long and not buying anything. Some of this stuff could be fun, right?"

"Oh!" I responded. "I mean, yes, yeah, let's do it." I'd assumed Grant would ignore the sex shop merch as much as possible. He's a modest midwesterner who didn't even kiss me until our fourth date. I'd almost given up the hope that they *were* dates until it happened, taking me by surprise almost as much as his suggesting that we buy a sex toy did four years later.

We reached for each other's hands and surveyed the contents of the brightly lit one-room store. Edible underwear in clear plastic casing, vibrators in every shape from egg to molar, virility candles, cock rings, costumes, handcuffs edged in purple fur, and dildos that ranged from the hyper-realistic to the holiday-themed. There was also a long shelf of books. I picked one up: *Hot Sex Tips, Tricks, and Licks*.

"Would you actually read that?" asked Grant. "I feel like it would just sit around our apartment."

"And then your parents would come visit and I'd hide it somewhere and forget all about it. You're right."

"What about edible underwear?"

"I don't know; it gets so sticky."

"Good call, let's try to avoid stuff that makes a mess. We don't want to be thinking about cleanup the whole time."

And so it went, us finding the work aspect of every item. We'd have to clean up the mango sex jelly, read a manual to figure out the Pleasure Periscope, train ourselves to enjoy BDSM in order to appreciate the *Fifty Shades of Grey*–inspired whip and cuff display. With each new discovery the bright excitement of deciding to buy something faded further into the dull arduousness of a task. We were no longer holding hands. I was scrutinizing the extensive caution label on a bottle of heat-activated massage oil and Grant was flipping through a book on tantra. "Man, you really have to learn another language," I heard him mutter. Everything in the store was designed for the sole purpose of turning us on, yet we'd had sexier experiences picking out ice cream at the corner bodega.

Fortunately I knew, according to Esther Perel—a sex therapist and the author of *Mating in Captivity*—that what we were experiencing wasn't a particular failing of ours but rather a symptom of a modern American issue: the Protestant work ethic getting all mixed up with sex. "This can-do attitude," writes Perel, "encourages us to assume that dwindling desire is an operational problem that can be fixed." On the mission to find hard and fast solutions to a problem that's as old as monogamy, we've invented the sex self-help book, libido-raising medications, the sex toy store, and the field of sex therapy. We've also invented the idea of collecting and publishing statistics that determine a "healthy" sex life—how many times per week, how long each session lasts, how many different moves are involved, and whether both partners reach climax. It's boring and stressful to think about sex this way, and thus ultimately counterproductive. Anyway, "you can't measure it," writes Perel. "Eroticism is inefficient . . . and imaginative."

I'd come across Perel's book in one of my Google searches (I think it was "monogamy spice sex expert help") and picked it up at the library one bright Tuesday afternoon. The semester had just ended and I was briefly between research clients, so I had the day free and was feeling weird about it. Usually my free time—weekends, holidays—is scheduled, often overly so. But this day had come upon me unawares: nothing on the calendar and everyone I knew was at work. A schoolteacher friend of mine back in San Diego used to leave his entire summers unplanned; I stopped by his house one afternoon, between my kayak guiding shift and my restaurant hostess shift, and found him lying in a patch of sun on the living room floor, shirtless and smiling, eyes closed, listening to music. I found it absolutely charming and completely incomprehensible. Five years later, wanting to emulate my relaxed friend but aware that I'd be antsy and annoyed after two unoccupied minutes in a sunbeam, I took Perel's book to the park. I'd make the most of my free day by learning while I relaxed.

Like the academic studies, Perel's book about the trials of monogamous sex focuses largely on boredom, but, unlike the academics, she offers solutions. This wasn't as comforting as I wanted it to be. She writes about the need for a "third" in a relationship, not necessarily an actual person but a fantasy or, more generally speaking, the ability to fantasize. "The third points to other possibilities, choices we didn't make," writes Perel, "and in this way it's bound up with our freedom." And freedom is sexy, while being trapped—or, as the title has it, "mating in captivity"—isn't.

Possibly I wasn't far enough removed from singlehood to appreciate this idea. I met Grant during a dry spell, something like three years after splitting with my college boyfriend, and while that time was peppered with dates and sexual encounters, I remember most of it as submerged in fantasy. This coincided with the recession, the same years that I was a kayak guide and a hostess, and while my sex life wasn't really boring, my jobs were—especially hostessing, which vies with dishwashing as the most tedious of restaurant jobs, especially during a recession, when people tend to eat out less. Alone and unoccupied, I'd lean against the hostess stand, not allowed to read or check my phone because it looked unprofessional, and daydream. All sorts of things went through my head— how I'd survive in a dystopia, what it would be like to live in a musical, whether a fake mustache would make me look tough enough to ensure my safety on a motorcycle trip through the Americas—but nine times out of ten they turned into a sexual fantasy. Given the risk of appearing even more unprofessional than I would by checking my phone, I couldn't whip out a vibrator, but otherwise my experience was consistent with research by the psychologist Kamel Gana and others, which found that "highly boredom prone individuals appeared more likely to be engaging in masturbatory experiences than low boredom prone individuals."

Did anyone know what I was daydreaming about back then? Could the customers or my coworkers tell just by looking? I gazed around the park, the sun making bright halos around the scattered forms of people napping or reading or tapping their phones, lending them an angelic air—no fantasies here. But maybe I just assumed that because I don't fantasize much anymore, and when I do it's about Grant. This was something I'd noticed before, and been proud of—it was like super-fidelity, an above-and-beyond proof of love, and I was annoyed with Perel for suggesting that I mix it up. I was annoyed, too, with the grass for tickling my ankles, with the man a couple of yards away talking loudly on his cell phone, with the roasted nut vendor who had just set up his stand on the sidewalk and was weighing down the fresh spring air with the heavy smells of oil and sugar, annoyed with all the "problems, simple, or impossible of solution," as James Baldwin put it, "to which the mind insanely clings in order to avoid the mind's real trouble."

Restlessness is part of me, so much so that I've taken to reading everything I can find about boredom, tedium, and the desire for novelty. I call it research because it sounds distant and professional, like the tastefully detached authors of all the studies in academic journals, but it's more personal than that, a quest for a cure more than anything else, and not in order to work harder but to love better. Watching a favorite author speak, my eyes might stray to my phone. Listening to a friend, my thoughts might wander. If I'm this bad at staying faithful to a conversation, how can I possibly remain faithful in a lifelong relationship? How can I trust myself not to hurt the person I love most?

It's not just simple restlessness that I fear. It takes a much larger lapse in self-control to sleep with someone than to check a phone. There are unthinking acts of boredom, like snacking or checking e-mail for the umpteenth time, and then there are deliberate dives into what seem like escape portals away from boredom. "At times an affair is a quest for intensity," Perel writes. Building a life together involves a certain amount of work, but "affairs unfold in the margins of our lives, and are luxuriously free of the dental appointments, taxes, and bills."

I'd actually experienced something like this, albeit secondhand. My college boyfriend and I split up over a spat about a late rent check that escalated into an argument about everything else, and it was only afterward that I found out he'd cheated on me. Like a stolen glance at an iPhone that the lecturing author doesn't catch, his interest had shifted even as I believed I held it. In the eyes of a man who'd loved me, I concluded, I'd become boring, "a radiating atom," as a character describes herself in Paul Murray's *Skippy Dies*, "the dull, decaying isotope of a lover." No wonder we'd split up. Boredom with a partner is often seen as a sign that they're just not the person for you, period. When a woman asked the *Washington Post* advice columnist if she should be concerned that she was finding her partner of two years boring, the columnist wrote a devastating two-line response (for the guy in that relationship, anyway): "You're bored. End of the line on this relationship, no?"

It took being cheated on to make me appreciate the gravity of the word "boring." Years later, this would help

me understand when Jeff Kling, the adman behind the
Dos Equis Most Interesting Man in the World campaign,
told me that an ex-girlfriend "used to say, jokingly, 'you bore
me,' and nothing made me more apoplectic." I knew what
it was like to look at myself on bad days and think, *you're
the worst, you stink, you're terrible.* But I'd never thought,
you're boring, and I never would have believed that boring
could be worse than terrible. Terrible is terrible. But boring
is . . . nothing. Unimportant. Insignificant. Forgettable.

The worst part is, this still doesn't protect you from
getting hurt. Being boring is seen as a character flaw, a
chronic inability to read the room, and we have very little
sympathy for boring people. It's more or less okay to avoid
them at parties, check texts while they speak, cut off their
stories, and even—especially online—out-and-out tell them
that they're boring: taking the time to log in to a website
comments section to write "meh" or "yawn" under an
article or a video, or veiling the insult in holier-than-thou
language like "homonormative," a word used by the film-
maker Ingrid Jungermann in a scene where a glamorous character puts down two thirtysomething, Indigo
Girls–loving gay women at a predominantly transgender
party. In the most extreme version of cruelty to the boring, an Australian teenager stabbed a friend of his to
death in 2015 because, as he texted to a common friend
of theirs in the week leading up to the murder, "he's so
boring" that "eliminating" him would be doing the world
a favor.

Being cheated on is obviously not as bad as being
killed. But it's definitely not something I want to inflict on

anyone else. Over the years when I was single and fantasizing about sex, the fear of being boring followed me
everywhere, along with the fear of being bored—because,
as many an Internet meme will tell you, only boring
people get bored. (Really, the statement contradicts itself.
If you think someone is boring, that means you're bored
by them, which would make *you* the boring one. This
could be a nice life lesson if not for the fact that real
life rarely works out that way—easily bored people tend
to be thrill-seekers, whereas those who lead stereo-
typically "boring" lives are apt to be quite content. As
Queen Elizabeth's party planner Lady Anson advises:
"Seat all the bores together. They don't realize they're the
bores, and they're happy.") From city to city, job to job,
guy to guy, I kept moving, collecting experiences like
trading cards to use as proof of my interestingness. Until
I met Grant.

We still hadn't found anything compelling in the sex shop.
"Should we call it?" Grant asked.

"Yeah, I've got nothing. Should we call it on trivia too?
It's been a while."

"Maybe five more minutes?" he suggested. I wasn't sure
whether he was actually eager for trivia or just worried
about hurting the saleswoman's feelings. She'd come over
to refill our drinks and apologize so many times that I'd
gotten a buzz and Grant had started saying, "No no, we
were early, let *me* apologize." Two minutes after we decided to stay, she sped over to us, her hands pressed tightly

together in anticipation as she announced: "It's time for trivia!"

We followed her to where the rest of the trivia group had gathered, about thirteen people. "Your trivia team is your life team!" chirped the saleswoman, which caused some confusion until we figured out that she meant each couple was its own team, so we didn't actually have to do anything. In the loose circle we'd formed in front of the saleswoman were two same-sex couples, three hetero, and a group of unpartnered goth girls who were probably below the drinking age.

"This is actually similar to a test I gave my middle schoolers today," said the saleswoman as she passed out pens and index cards. "I should mention," she added, "that I teach sex ed. Anyway, just write your team name on an index card. When I have everyone's, we'll start."

"I hope this isn't like middle school sex ed," whispered Grant.

"It can't be. I can't imagine anything less sexy."

"Or grosser."

"My middle school sex ed teacher had no cartilage in his nose. He used to squish it down to show us. I'll forever associate that image with the word 'vulva.'"

"Ugh, that's terrible. Who thought the word 'vulva' was a good idea? It's almost as bad as—"

"Are you two all set with a team name?" asked the saleswoman, suddenly right in front of us.

"Yes, sorry, just a sec." Grant wrote something down and showed it to me. I snorted, then shrugged. "Works for me. Or I guess the joke would be that it doesn't. Bah dum cha."

The saleswoman took our card and walked back up to the front to announce our team names. The goth girls to our left were Whips 'n' Tits. A preppie-looking couple to our right was Up All Night. And in the middle was us, Lake Flaccid. Nobody laughed. Grant exhaled resignedly. "Misfire," he whispered, and before I could stop myself I whispered: "That's what she said." Everything was a dick joke now. We'd stayed too long at the sex shop.

Bad jokes were what first brought us together. When we met, Grant was a postproduction supervisor at *The Onion* and I was an editorial intern. Neither of us was tasked with actually being funny, but, like everyone else in the office, we were often used as joke sounding boards, sometimes unwittingly. A line that got a good laugh by the coffee-maker might wind up in more polished form as a head-line in the next week's issue. It really raised the stakes of conversation. In the midst of all this high-quality banter, Grant mostly listened and laughed, but when he joked he favored dad jokes. This was surprising, given our environment, and I found it comforting. For better or worse, there are few things that say "at ease with myself" more than the telling of a dad joke. Deliberately unfunny and derivative, the dad joke takes its name from men who've lived with their partners and kids for so long that they've put aside or maybe even forgotten the "seemingly common adult fear of being boring," in the words of Adam Phillips. "Once a man has children," quipped Jerry Seinfeld, "for the rest of his life his attitude is: the hell with the world, I can make my own people. I'll eat whatever I want, I'll wear whatever I want . . ." *I'll tell whatever jokes I want, regardless of how predictable they are.*

But Grant didn't have kids or a partner, and his ease distinguished him from me and my fellow single people—all of us wanting so badly to seem interesting. This took different forms, the most blatant example being one man I dated briefly whose business card listed his name, his phone number, and the word "Adventurer," along with an illustration of a pirate ship that was inexplicably on fire. Less blatant but more disturbing, another guy kept finding ways to mention the faint possibility that he was part Navajo— "my great-grandmother, according to my uncle, which is why I got this feather tattoo"—and it was painful to see him lean so hard on this dubious heritage, as if he had so little trust in his own ability to be interesting that he'd felt the need to co-opt a whole identity from another culture.

More typically, dates found ways to mention their hobbies, travel, eclectic music tastes, and any cool aspects of their careers as often as possible. There were also plenty of jokes, or attempts at jokes, some of them mine. Not being funny is a huge stumbling block in the dating world. You ask someone what they want, ten to one "someone who makes me laugh" is second only to "someone who turns me on." Being funny is so important that it's often positioned as roughly antithetical to being boring. As Aziz Ansari writes in his study of dating, *Modern Romance*, you either say something that "makes you seem like a pretty boring generic person" or you "say something thoughtful or funny."

Ansari's book is particularly concerned with online dating, which has upped the pressure to be interesting by both widening the pool of possibilities and lowering the value of subtlety. On the Internet nearly everyone is well traveled and well read, successful and active with a busy social life that affords novelties at every turn. According to a 2014 *Wired* study, some of the most common phrases in the most successful online profiles are "passport," "surfing," "holidays," "flying," "exploring," "vacations," "new places," "trying new things," "meeting new people," and "something new." This speaks less about who we are than about what we want: people can lie on their profiles—half of all online daters in Britain and the United States do, according to a 2012 study, and *Wired* cautioned that some of the most popular hobbies, such as surfing and yoga, might be "aspirational"—but the data on what we're most apt to click on doesn't lie. Apparently we want the adventurers, the thrill-seekers, people who are always doing new things and might bring us along for the ride, making our lives feel new too. That the people who seek thrills are, by definition, the people who are most easily bored doesn't seem to be a consideration.

The thing about everyone seeming interesting is that interesting starts to seem boring after a while, or at least like something with too many predictable parts. When everyone is talking about exploring and surfing and meeting new people, the whole thing starts to lose appeal.

This is where purely photo-based services such as Tinder might seem like a solution, but they're really just more of the same: pictures of single people backpacking through Europe or doing headstands on beaches or standing next to sculptures making goofy faces that say, "I'm cultured because I go to museums but cool because I don't take art too seriously." We're fit, we're fun, we're funny—love us. I wasn't even online dating and I was still doing the same thing, pulling from my trusty arsenal of eclectic jobs and moves to impress dates, practically daring them to find me, who'd worked on the farm of a Spanish anarchist *and* been a lobbyist in the Missouri House of Representatives, boring. But we were all in the same boat, all boring one another with our fascinating selves, except, it seemed, for Grant, whose seeming indifference to the topic of his own interestingness made him the most interesting guy I'd met in a long time.

Somehow it all worked out. He liked me back, and our first kiss was supercharged with four dates of anticipation. We fell in love, we moved in together, and eventually we were standing side-by-side in a sex shop, Team Lake Flaccid, listening attentively as a middle school sex ed teacher asked, "What was the most commonly reported male fantasy in 2000?"

"Britney Spears," whispered Grant confidently.

"Really?" I hadn't pegged Grant as a Britney guy. Instinctively I reached to touch my hair. In terms of length, it was closer to Britney's bald dome of 2007 than to her long locks of 2000. I'd been wondering if he had a "third," in Perel parlance: a non-me fantasy. Was it still Britney?

"Sure. Wasn't that the year she was on the cover of *Rolling Stone* in her underwear?"

"I guess so. Sometime around then anyway. And it made a big deal out of her being a sexy teenager. As a preteen girl I remember finding that cover really creepy."

"Yeah, I can see that. As a teenage guy I just thought it was hot."

"So you had a Britney Spears thing. We've never talked about this."

"Well, it wasn't an especially unique attraction at the time. I think I was pretty average."

"Then I guess Britney is probably the right answer." I shook my head as I wrote it down on our index card, which the saleswoman came around to collect. Britney wasn't so bad; there were more intimidating things he could have said. Like . . .

"Threesomes," read the saleswoman from an index card, ". . . is correct! Congratulations, Team Up All Night— and you're actually the only team to get a point this round."

Groans all around. "I thought threesomes were passé?" I heard one of the teen goths to our left whisper. "Maybe not in 2000," one of her friends whispered back. On our right, the female half of Team Up All Night stroked her partner's be-Dockered butt and bit her lip. He kissed her just above her pearls. They were proving themselves worthy of their team name; I didn't want to seem worthy of ours. I put an arm around Grant's waist, and he put one around my shoulders. He turned toward me. I leaned in expectantly. He brought his lips close to my ear, and he whispered: "I kind of feel bad for Britney, don't you?" I straightened up and sighed. "Yeah. Poor Britney."

"Adding a third is not for everyone," the polyamorist and psychologist Deborah Anapol told me. "You have to really communicate to find out if it is, otherwise people feel abandoned."

Anapol wasn't talking about a fantasy. In an effort to come to terms with Perel's suggestion of an imagined third, I'd decided to explore something even scarier: the idea of an actual flesh-and-blood addition to a relationship. The idea came from a conversation with a New York–based couples therapist, Sylvia Rosenfeld, who told me that some people are just "naturally hard-wired to want more novelty" than other people, and while this can cause problems in a relationship, it doesn't have to. "There are a lot of people who like novelty in the polyamory community, for example," she said. "They seek it intentionally and with agreement, and that makes a difference."

Polyamory was so far outside my comfort zone that talking about it didn't faze me nearly as much as Perel's advice, which cut too close to the bone. Further research led me to Anapol, who was honored as one of America's leading experts and practitioners of polyamory upon her death, less than a year after we spoke. She explained that at the beginning of a romance there's a rush of what she calls "new relationship energy," which naturally fades over time. Serial monogamists jump from one relationship energy rush to the next. Lifelong monogamists do without the rush, or cheat. Polyamorists typically stay committed to their "primary partner" while simultaneously seeking the rush with other people. "At some level everyone needs novelty," said Anapol, but, she added—as if she could tell polyamory wasn't something I was really considering—it doesn't have to come from a new person. "There are plenty of other ways to find novelty. Talking about sex really helps, at a couples retreat or one-on-one with your partner, sharing your fantasies."

There we were, back where I'd begun, though in comparison with polyamory fantasizing wasn't quite so threatening anymore. Maybe if my ex and I had fantasized more, and talked more about our fantasies with each other, he wouldn't have grown bored. I couldn't even be sure, looking back, if that's what had actually happened. He might not have been bored but rather angry, or lonely, or scared, or in love with the other woman, however briefly. And if he *was* bored, it wasn't necessarily with me. One of Esther Perel's clients, for example, was experiencing a "feeling of deadness" when he developed a crush on his wife's friend. "I'm in love with my wife," he told Perel; "this has nothing to do with her. It's about something I've lost that I'm afraid I'll never get back."

It's not a particularly comforting anecdote, but monogamy isn't a particularly comfortable state. We decide to spend years of our lives with one person, whose body we might get to know but whose self we can never fully uncover, and that's incredibly unnerving. I didn't know what motivated my ex, and I don't really know what motivates Grant, whose fondness for dad jokes and sympathy with Britney Spears are only attributes, things that I can observe and question and theorize about but that will only ever take me so far into his psyche. We could talk about fantasies for hours and I still wouldn't know what thoughts run through his head while he's riding the train, what sadness feels like for him, or what he sees when he looks at the color blue. He can't know those things about me either, and there are even more things we don't know about ourselves, ways in which we'll interact and change each other over the years. There is so much we don't and cannot know. Researchers can present us with data and studies but they have no solutions for what the writer Elif Batuman calls "the problem of person."

At another time these thoughts might have made me feel lonely—the idea that nobody will ever completely know me, or I them, and that no amount of research can change this—but, given that boredom was my pressing concern, it came as a small relief. None of us is quite as fathomable as we hope, or as predictable as we fear, even to ourselves. It's possible that the same is true of monogamy: that it's actually for the best that we don't have it all figured out. At any rate it keeps us on our toes.

I don't think anyone was shocked when Team Lake Flaccid didn't win sexy trivia, though the goth teens of Team Whips 'n' Tits did seem surprised to have placed behind us. It turned out not to really matter who won or lost because each team received mini silver vibrators just for participating. On our way out I flicked ours on and tested it on Grant's arm. "Ouch, damn, are you really supposed to put that right on your bare skin?"

"Yeah, that's how they work."

"Well, be careful," Grant said, rubbing his arm. "You could burn something off."

"An unsexy parting gift for an unsexy evening."

"I don't know, I had fun," said Grant as we stepped out into the starless night, the street as dark as it ever gets in the city, streetlights and bar signs and the glow of apartment windows.

"You did?"

"Yeah, didn't you?" He linked his arm with mine as we walked to our subway stop. "It's good to talk about that stuff."

"But weird, right?"

"Definitely weird. But good, I think. And hey, you never told me, what was your fantasy in 2000?"

"You want to know a preteen's fantasies? That's pretty pervy."

"*You* know *mine*. Anyway, you should tell me because otherwise I'll say that word . . ."

"Ugh, gross—no!"

"Vulv—"

I kissed him. He kissed me back. And there we were, making out on the street like a couple who doesn't live together in an apartment where they can kiss in private as much as they want. *It won't always be like this*, I thought to myself. And then another thought: *You really have no idea what's going to happen.*

3

BORED IN BAGHDAD

Everybody had their own ways of coping," said Sergeant Brian Turner about the stretches of boredom he endured as a soldier. For many, "it was often porn."

It was the second time in a week that porn and war had come up in the same conversation. We'd had dinner with our neighbors, a retired naval officer and his wife, and he'd told us that most of his men boarded submarines armed with "laptops chock-full of porn" to while away weeks without wives or Wi-Fi. At the time I hadn't questioned it; a couple of weeks is a long time to spend in tight quarters, no connection to the rest of the world, so it just made sense to pack a laptop full of distractions. Plus, I'd recently read a study about boredom and masturbation. They're highly correlated, but neither the study nor our neighbor had speculated as to why.

"Why porn, specifically?"

"A need for intimacy," Brian answered immediately. "It's not really intimate, of course. But it's an imaginative act. And in that sense, it doesn't have to be porn. I listened to a lot of music. It could be anything—anything that transports you away from where you are."

The "where" for Brian was Iraq in the aughts, patrolling for terrorists in the heat and dust but mostly waiting, according to Brian's book, *My Life as a Foreign Country*. It's a catalog of boredom coping mechanisms: the soldiers listen to music, tell stories, watch movies, get in fights, look at porn, and buy things to help fill the time, "like the cheap, flat black throwing knives which we fling at the trunks of palm trees to whittle away our boredom." Always there was "the hovering presence of anxiety and adrenaline," which physical activities, such as throwing knives and organizing a boxing tournament, were especially helpful in dispelling.

The more I read about war, the more I found that the "where" doesn't really make much difference as far as boredom goes. Brian and his fellow soldiers might as well have been in Kuwait, arguing and masturbating with the marines in Anthony Swofford's *Jarhead*, or in Israel, having sex and talking about sex and daydreaming about shooting off his own leg just for something to do like the soldiers in Shani Boianjiu's *The People of Forever Are Not Afraid*. The when isn't even all that important: according to the World War II veteran Paul Fussell, his companions learned to fill their free time with naps because "sleep devours boredom," and they wrote massive amounts of letters and journals for the same reason. Some of them also wrote books, which piled up on my nightstand along with the rest, a hodge-podge of reminiscences that all seemed to want to communicate one thing: war isn't as exciting as you think.

I'd never intended to read so many books about war. I didn't really want to read *any* books about war, if I could help it—I'd seen heaps of action movies over the last few years with Grant, and had grown weary of blood and epic battles. When Thor, Iron Man, and Captain America all descended on the bad guy in the middle of a huge metropolis full of screaming civilians, that was my cue to get a popcorn refill, avoiding what the movie critic Matt Zoller Seitz calls "the enervating sight of huge things crashing into other huge things." This meant I was usually ducking out of the theater during any scenes that had life-and-death consequences, and there was something shameful about this; it seemed like the act of an unfeeling person, or at least an unserious one, someone who doesn't want to know or doesn't care that such scenes are meant to represent War with a capital *W*, which is always happening somewhere around the world. Violence is tedious only to those of us lucky to live far away from real war, untouched by the fear that one of those huge things crashing around might crash into us. Or at least that's what I thought before coming across a 2004 interview with several Baghdadi teen boys whose chief complaint about the War on Terror that had landed in their city was that it had made their lives boring.

Their streets were under constant threat of bombing and patrolled night and day by armed soldiers, who held the whole city to a nine o'clock curfew. The teens couldn't go out with their friends and even their graduation party was rescheduled for mid-afternoon and then cut short. Those who could afford to emigrate were leaving, and as the rest neared adulthood they dreaded the claustrophobic lack of options in the locked-down and bombed-out city that they called home. I was surprised by how little they sounded like the victims or heroes in movies. They sounded like real people I might know, frustrated and aimless and trapped, reminding me more than anything else of the boys I grew up with in northern Indiana.

We were also teenagers in 2004, and though we knew a few soldiers who'd gone to Iraq we were physically very far away from the War on Terror, just as we had been from the events of 9/11. Parents and teachers reminded us that we were lucky to live in a safe and quiet place, which was undeniably true, but we were all still clearly agitated by the faraway drama, unnerved by the disconnect between the quiet lives we lived and the distant chaos we saw unfold on television. In Iraq, violence created an atmosphere of boredom. At the same time, in my hometown all the way across the world, boredom created an atmosphere of violence. Fights broke out in our school hallways and groups of boys drove down the streets bashing mailboxes with baseball bats. I don't actually know whether this had anything to do with the war or whether teen boys are always like that and the war was just a narrative coincidence, a way to link these actions to the rest of the world, which was so much bigger than us and so hard to touch.

It's probably the latter. Statistically speaking, restless violence is the purview of teen boys—they are the ones most likely to wrestle for fun, destroy property out of boredom, or even kill an animal or person solely for excitement, a class of murder known as a "thrill kill." The girls I grew up with dealt with small-town confinement differently: we entangled ourselves in epic romances and got into convoluted nonphysical fights with one another that might last for days. When we see one another now we laugh at the drama of our younger selves, but at the time we took it very seriously, never attributing it to boredom like our male counterparts did.

All this has historical precedence. As the boredom scholar Patricia Meyer Spacks writes, "In women's novels of the eighteenth century, boredom characteristically belongs mainly to men, sometimes as a cultivated stance. Misery—exaggerated, complicated misery—replaces boredom as a female experience in these fictions. Eighteenth-century conduct books for women make it clear that females who admit to boredom thereby violate an important standard." At the time, she explains, most women's lives unfolded in the confines of the home—laundry, cooking, and housework for the lower classes, obligatory leisure for the upper classes—and thus lacked the opportunities for variety, novelty, and action that men's lives had, whether that entailed hustling in the city markets, participating in politics, or traveling the world with the military. Women still had to somehow hold the interest of the men who supported them, so they worked with what they had, because "a woman has the obligation to make herself interesting."

I thought this might have been why my friends and I were reluctant to talk about boredom when we were younger, and it seemed possible that my weariness with action movies—along with contact sports and war history books, all marketed mostly to men—might come from a similar place, a historically constructed idea of how a woman *should* be. It's good that I no longer avoid thinking about boredom, because, despite what my younger self wanted to believe, at least a few of those earlier dramas really *did* unfold because my friends and I were a bit bored, and this realization has actually been a huge relief. Not only that, but the more I learn about boredom, the more useful that understanding proves to be, providing extra signage to guide me safely through the minefields of adulthood. It seemed possible that there were similar lessons in war stories that I was missing by avoiding them, something to be learned by paying attention to the staged battles in movies and reading about the experiences of soldiers and civilians like the Iraqi teens, whose boredom in the midst of war had piqued my interest in the first place. In *The Godfather*, which I finally saw in my late twenties at Grant's behest, the Mafia resolves issues by going to the mattresses. In more subdued and much less cinematically compelling fashion, I went to the books.

I went first for the volume most directly marketed to me, a literary novel about war from a woman's perspective. Shani Boianjiu is an Israeli who served her two mandatory years in the army after high school and later wrote

The People of Forever Are Not Afraid, about a group of teen
girl soldiers. Her characters' complaints felt familiar to
me in the same way that those of the Iraqi boys did. They
grew up in a small town where airplane parts are made;
I grew up in a small town where Hummer parts are
made. As soldiers they're often bored but they find things
to obsess and gossip about together, like my high school
friends and I did. "We were all killing time," writes Boianjiu, "and at the end of the day every person liked to talk
about just one thing. For my new room," she adds, "it
was sex." The glaring difference between us was that
I grew up in the American Midwest and these soldiers
lived in the Middle East, the former as isolated from
warfare as it could be, the latter so regularly rocked by
violence for so many decades that, for Boianjiu's characters,
it's normal.

The book is great, unique and absorbing if very bleak,
but what astonished me even more than the book itself
was the outsized anger of online commenters who'd taken
to Amazon or Goodreads to tell Boianjiu, and the rest
of the world, exactly how much they hated reading the
dialogue of soldiers "whining about boyfriends, school
friends, and other teenager-y concerns," in the words of
someone going by the name "lh422." "I felt like I was
reading the diary of a teenager," wrote someone going by
"asher," who presumably meant this as an insult, since on
that basis he or she gave this book—which is about and
narrated by teenagers—just one star, the minimum re-
quired in order to be able to publish a review on Amazon.
Another commenter, going by "rvearl," claimed to have

been so mad that he or she actually threw the book on the ground and then "seriously considered not taking the book back to the library just to save others from squandering their time." They were disappointed in the book for the very reason I'd sought it out: it's not a traditional war narrative, "replete with adventures and a dénouement," in the words of a disappointed "sharon beverly." They'd wanted heroes and villains and victims, but instead they found regular bored teenagers who just happened to grow up in an atmosphere of violence and death.

Obviously, ringing Boianjiu's doorbell and reading these comments would be unquestionably cruel, pointlessly unkind, but angry reviews such as these have become so normal online that you can now quickly and easily find a diatribe against just about everything, from a book to a piece of fish to a complete stranger's political opinions. These comments range from mildly unkind to scary, such as those found under an article in the U.K.'s *Daily Express* about complaints of boredom from Syrian refugees, who had fled ISIS and were stuck in indefinite limbo in encampments all over Europe. "Drop a bomb on the camps" was the most out-and-out violent comment I came across, suggested by someone going by the moniker "janoli." More regularly, the commenters expressed variations of the declaration made by "mistermac": "There is a simple answer for these ungrateful people—they can sod off back to where they came from."

Similar to the outrage against the characters in Boianjiu's novel, these commenters' anger seems to stem from the perception that if the refugees were truly thankful to be alive they wouldn't feel bored, despite the fact that they're not allowed to work and they spend hours each day waiting in lines for food, medical service, and legal advice. By being bored, they're not playing their victim role correctly, not being the indebted damsels in distress.

But if the possibility of impending death is all it takes, then, really, none of us should experience boredom. We all know we're going to die and we rarely know how we'll go. We risk our lives daily just by walking down the street, some more than others, depending on where we live and who we are, but even the substantial insulation of wealth and whiteness doesn't prevent somebody from getting hit by a car or lightning or an unexpected heart attack. A girl I grew up with lost her father when a tornado passed through town and his office caved in. Before that, we'd all been so blasé toward the frequency of tornadoes in the Midwest that we often used the unoccupied time during school tornado drills to paint our nails; even afterward it didn't take long for most of us to go back to that same old habit—after all, what were the odds of it happening again? "Life is intrinsically, well, boring and dangerous at the same time," as the artist Edward Gorey put it. "At any given moment the floor may open up. Of course, it almost never does; that's what makes it so boring." We might unknowingly pass within an inch of death four times during the morning commute and still be preoccupied with petty concerns, such as how annoying those female soldier characters were in that book we read on the train, and how good it's going to feel to log in to Amazon once we get to the office and write a one-star review.

We probably should all be grateful and energized just by being alive, but mostly we don't think about it—the very existence of angry online commenters is just further proof of that. In a study of four thousand cases, the linguist Claire Hardaker found that boredom was one of the chief motivations for online bullying, along with feeling disenfranchised. These feelings are often found together, since "being trapped in an unwanted situation," in the words of the psychologist John Eastwood, "is one of the hallmarks of boredom." I read this in a study of Eastwood's and thought again of being a teenager, so close to adulthood but still so limited as to what you can actually do, unable to choose where you live or how you spend much of your time or even, depending on where you grow up, whether or not you'll serve in the military. Teenagers are more likely than adults to vocally complain about boredom, and perhaps for this reason it's often assumed that the typical Internet bully is a teen, but Hardaker says there is no "typical troll." People of all backgrounds and ages choose to vent their frustrations online, men and women both, attempting to exorcise the civilian's version of the soldier's "hovering presence of anxiety and adrenaline" by engaging in violence of a different sort, casual and covert and capable of being committed in pajamas.

Thinking about the nonphysical brutality of Internet trolls as a form of violence made it easier to understand the

bored person's draw toward violence in general. I'd engaged in this nonphysical form myself, letting unwanted
inertia make me mean and apt to snap over just about
anything. Living, during the recession, in San Diego—a
town I'd never thought about until I moved there for my
college boyfriend, but where I remained, slowly saving
money to move elsewhere (though I wasn't sure where
or even why), for a year after we split—gave me plenty of
opportunity to unleash my restless anxiety on strangers
via road rage, muttering inaudibly at motorists who drove
too slow or too fast or didn't use their signals, shouting
curses at anyone who veered too close or cut me off. Unfortunately, the only mode of transportation I'd been able
to afford on my restaurant salary was a motor scooter,
which made me the least intimidating person on the road,
my pip-squeak fury eliciting laughter from the occupants
of actual cars.

According to the boredom scholar Seán Desmond
Healy, when we're bored our "nerves are stretched, it
seems, beyond the breaking point—but for no definite,
identifiable reason—and hence beyond the reach of any
conceivable salve," leading us to act out in "exasperated
violence." In my experience, there usually *is* a reason,
but it's too global or complicated to be able to articulate
without some work, and too uncomfortable to think
about for as long as it would take to figure it out. When
the problem involves exploring such sticky concepts as
meaning or powerlessness, it's easier to just blame it on
traffic or breakups or the faults of an author we've never
met or, if pressed, on stress or boredom—both bucket

words we use to hold a whole spectrum of unspoken and unspeakable concerns. When three Oklahoma teens, for example, shot a stranger in 2013 because they "were bored and didn't have anything to do," what exactly was happening for them? Were they feeling the same fear of inertia, of the same unlovable hustle every day until death, that made me act like such a laughable jerk toward San Diego's commuters? Or were they feeling something completely different? In the same way that I can't know exactly what Grant sees when he looks at the color blue, I can't really know the nuances of anyone else's motives for bored violence, physical or otherwise.

Which is not to say that plenty of experts haven't tried. The psychologist and Holocaust survivor Erich Fromm hypothesized that boredom-induced violence stemmed from the ways that our economic system uses and abuses people. Many people have to spend the majority of their lives doing work they don't care about, for employers who may or may not treat them fairly, and the rest of us live in a world where we know that's happening—that the smartphones that entertain us are made in sweatshops, the sugar that sweetens our cakes and coffees harvested by underpaid laborers—but don't know what to do about it. Or maybe we don't really want to do anything about it, I don't know; if enough of us really *did* want to shut down the system, it seems like we would have done it by now. Instead, we give our tacit consent through the purchases we make to prevent boredom. It's all part of the violent aura cast by capitalism, according to Fromm. "Exploitation and manipulation produce boredom and triviality," he wrote. "They cripple man, and all factors that make man into a psychic cripple turn him also into a sadist or a destroyer."

The anthropologist Ernest Becker thought the problem went even deeper and further back than capitalism, finding the root for all violence—really, human behavior in general, capitalism included—in our fear of death. The thrill killer, he argued, attempts to reclaim power over death by wielding it. "I am threatened by death," he quoted an imaginary killer as saying; "let us kill plentifully." Murder is also a way to achieve some kind of immortality through notoriety. Everyone wants to be some kind of hero, argued Becker, because we all want our lives to be significant, but if heroism doesn't seem possible some people would prefer villainy to obscurity. At least you get to be at the center of a story, even if it's a horror story.

I think I would have balked at this—we *all* want to be heroes? really?—if I hadn't come across Becker while immersed in the world of war stories. Staring up at a screen night after night, I watched men and women (mostly men) save lives, save countries, save the world. They usually seemed to do these things because they had to, they'd had greatness gracefully thrust upon them, but you had to wonder what would have happened to them if they were like the rest of us: working regular jobs and coming home to sit on the couch, or going out to sit in a darkened theater, in order to live vicariously through someone *else* becoming a hero. If greatness didn't come knocking, would they seek it out? How? Would they cruise restaurants looking for someone who needs the Heimlich and bridges looking for someone who might jump? Would they hit the streets to exercise vigilante justice on presumed bad guys? Would they sneak away from home like the Marquis de Lafayette and his friends, leaving France to join the American rebellion because they were "tired of the *longeur* of the peace that had lasted ten years"? Or would they go to their local recruitment office, like Brian Turner, who "joined the infantry because at some point in the hero's life the hero is supposed to say 'I swear'"?

This was why I'd reached out to Brian in the first place: because he so frankly addressed the desire to be a hero, which Becker says we all feel but usually try to suppress. We might "disguise our struggle by piling up figures in a bank book to reflect privately our sense of heroic worth," he wrote. Or we adopt a cause to fight for, a need that may help explain how cause-worthy situations—such as the plight of sweatshop workers—rarely seem to actually improve. "Be wary," wrote the activist DeRay Mckesson, "of those that are addicted to struggle more than they are in love with freedom." For some, it might be preferable for there to be victims and struggle, rather than peace and purposelessness. World leaders, from Churchill to Bush Senior, have described the excitement of war as preferable to the more prosaic tasks of peacetime.

But most commonly we distract ourselves: with interpersonal dramas, busywork, watching movies and reading books about fictional heroes, writing scathing comments online, being angry or annoyed—even self-administering electric shocks is preferable to being unoccupied and alone with our thoughts, according to a 2014 study. We hate being bored in part because our unoccupied minds might wander over to the uncomfortable issue of what we're doing to cope with our mortality. Yet "becoming conscious of what one is doing to earn his feelings of heroism," writes Becker, "is the main self-analytic problem of life."

Even just trying to think in these terms made me blush. The word "hero" is embarrassing: so grand as to sound immature, something out of an adolescent daydream, like when I used to imagine myself as Juliet and my high school boyfriend as Romeo because being star-crossed would imbue our new love with more importance. But it didn't come off as immature when Brian addressed it, perhaps because the military has a built-in tradition of heroism. War is where the notions of honor and glory originated, tracing all the way back to Homer's *Iliad*, when Hector dives into battle, knowing he's going to die but determined to "first do some great thing that shall be told among men hereafter." When you enter a combat zone, explained Brian, "the potential in front of you is already layered with historic moments."

"What does that mean, exactly?"

"You don't have to work so hard to feel like part of something," he explained. "Usually we have to climb a sort of metaphorical tree and pluck from it to find meaning, but at war it's falling on your head." Ever since he wrote about his time in Iraq, he added, self-proclaimed pacifists have been approaching him furtively, "always off to the side," to confess secret longings to go to war. They tell him they don't want to miss this historic moment, or that they're itching for a chance to do something more meaningful with their lives.

This was something I could understand. As far as grand concepts go, meaning is a more socially acceptable thing to want than heroism, but at the end of the day they're more or less the same thing. While I was doing work that didn't mean anything to me in San Diego, a place I'd never meant to live, it felt as if I'd slipped out of the role of protagonist in my own life, just fallen right out of the story altogether—a roundabout civilian way of saying I was failing to earn my feelings of heroism. And this failure made me mean.

Violence is a bid for power: during the recession I might not have been able to find a better job, but I *could* pawn my bad mood off onto a turn-signal-neglecting stranger. In this sense, it serves as both a response to a lack of meaning and, in the form of war, an avenue through which to achieve meaning. The latter has the clear focus—*these are the bad guys, our job is to get them*—and social sanction that the former lacks, which in turn suggests an explanation for the lasting appeal of war stories, from the *Iliad* to *The Avengers*: they make being a hero seem like a straightforward process. Not easy, per se, but clear. You show up, shake the hand of your new commander, put on your new uniform, and you're on your way, bound for a life where high-stakes heroism is no longer an embarrassing adolescent preoccupation, but a real possibility.

This gave me more appreciation for war movies in general, but still I found the fight scenes in movies boring.

I'd been talking to friends—women who like fight scenes, men who don't, and vice versa, with no rhyme or reason—and had begun to suspect that my dislike of fight scenes has less to do with my gender and more to do with the simple fact that I'm easily bored. I enjoyed Brian's and Boianjiu's books about bored soldiers not because they're less violent (they aren't) but because they're different. They are less exciting but more engaging, maybe because, like the bored teens in Baghdad, their characters aren't superhuman heroes but more like people I know: unsure, often bored, just trying to figure it all out.

Oddly enough, this thought gave me more sympathy for all the Internet commenters who *don't* like such books. It was possible that their complaints reflected a deeper disappointment than simple frustration with someone else's lack of gratitude. War books and movies often imply that just being near violence and death, then escaping, carries you permanently above mundane human concerns, cruising at altitude, completely and unfailingly satisfied ever after. These stories are inspiring because they offer hope that we can all transcend the stupid stuff, and it's disheartening to find that it doesn't always work out that way: kids growing up in war-torn areas still complain, adults who've escaped still get annoyed when they have nothing to do, and even active soldiers still mess around on the Internet looking for porn.

Thinking back to youthful boredom, playing out in romantic drama or road rage, I actually appreciate the dream-deflating aspects of these stories. It's a strange comfort to know that longing never goes away, even when you're *in* the movie, so to speak. These stories suggest that, like sunshine, meaning probably isn't something you find and then just sit in its glow, completely fulfilled forever. Clouds obscure it momentarily; night falls and takes it away completely for a while. Meaning is unpredictable: it might go away anytime—leaving us bored and weary of a tedious world—but it might also come back anytime, when we're on the battlefield or in traffic, waiting for the light to change.

4

THOMAS COOK
AND THE STACK PIRATES

On a July bank holiday in 1841, about four hundred people arrived at the Loughborough train station with tickets for Thomas Cook's first tour. It was a modest excursion: eleven miles from one English village to another, where they'd have a picnic of the squeaky-clean *Anne of Green Gables* variety—games, lemonade, tea and cakes—then back home. Bridges along the way were packed with people watching the vacationers' train speed down the track.

The year 1841 had already been one of firsts for English travel. Between January and July, Britain occupied Hong Kong and colonized New Zealand, David Livingstone (of "Dr. Livingstone, I presume") arrived at his first African post, and the explorer James Clark Ross braved Antarctic temperatures to discover an ice shelf the size of France. Amid all this to-ing and fro-ing and building of empire,

I doubt many people in 1841 were thinking, *Wow, that tour guide Thomas Cook, with his picnics and cheap train tickets, he's going to be the one to shape the world*. Yet today Thomas Cook is regarded as the father of tourism.

Tourism, now one of the world's biggest industries, began as the personal mission of a zealot. Cook had taken the temperance pledge at twenty-five and dedicated his life to converting others, a mission that shaped his career and perhaps his physiognomy: his granddaughter described him as having "the black piercing eyes of a fanatic." He'd grown up in a working-class town, the kind of community in which drinking was the primary leisure activity, and, as one nineteenth-century clergyman describes, "a visit to a distant market town is an achievement to render a man an authority or an oracle among his brethren, and one who has accomplished that journey twice or thrice is ever regarded as a daring traveler." Aristocrats and nobles traveled the world, but few regular people had ever been out of their hometowns. The vast majority of English men and women had never seen London.

Cook, however, had begun his career as an intervillage missionary. While wandering the dusty roads between towns, he'd observed his own feelings of exhilaration at seeing new places, as well as the shared tedium of his countrymen's lives: doing the same things, seeing the same things, every day. This, he began to believe, was what they were trying to escape by drinking—then the drinking itself became one of the habits they could not escape. With the advent of passenger trains, Cook saw an opportunity for "lifting them out of the dull round of everyday life." He arranged a package deal so that individual tickets were affordable and remade himself as a tour guide.

"No two movements are more closely affiliated," wrote Cook of temperance and tourism. When one thinks about spring breakers ordering buckets of beer in Cancún and retirees getting tipsy on Caribbean cruises, Cook's surety is funny and a little sad. Yet his theory of why travel *should* contribute to temperance still rings true. We grow restless in static lives. We create habits to make tedium bearable, but unvaried habits eventually become part of the same old: morning coffee, smoke break, happy hour. This is why we need travel, which, according to Cook, "helps to pull men out of the mire and pollution of old corrupt customs."

I learned all this from Cook's biography, which I read on the ninth floor of the Columbia library stacks, sipping the coffee I'd snuck in. I sipped in plain sight because the only other person around to care—a squat gray-haired man with a black patch over his left eye—didn't. We know each other, kind of, as we're often the only people up here. He's probably an alum, like me, milking our lifetime access to one of the few quiet places in Manhattan. His focus is better than mine: he reads court records all day, spine curved and one finger following the type, never getting up, not even to go to the bathroom, though an enormous plastic cup of iced tea sweats in front of him (smuggling that in is a serious accomplishment). Occasionally he asks me the time, though it doesn't seem to have any bearing on what he does.

In contrast, I'm up and down all day. Going to get a book. Going to the lobby to use my phone. Going out to get a snack that I have to sneak back in. Crossing and uncrossing my legs. Sighing. My mom has the same restlessness, a symptom of anxiety, for which she joined a support group. They have a phone tree, and when one of them is anxious they call one of the others. These calls have become a source of great anxiety for my mom.

She's a hospital nurse, which is a good use of all her nervous energy. I like research for the same reason: it's a lot of walking around looking for books and talking to people. Still, I manage to get distracted. I found Cook's biography because I'd gotten bored with the books I'd gathered on boredom, left my coffee to cool and the old man to figure out the time on his own, and wandered down to the travel section of the stacks.

I was thinking of taking a trip, though I didn't have any money. Fortunately, the travel section of a college library is a terrible place to plan a vacation. It's all biographies and histories and outdated research. Here in the murky deep-sea gloom of the stacks, Ukraine is in the U.S.S.R., Istanbul is Constantinople, Louisiana has yet to be purchased, and the ground I stand on is empty air above a small green island, where coyote stalk prey and bears hibernate. I like these books. The further back the narrative, the fresher the world seems, the sins of our fathers confined to their limited range.

Cook's biography is the story of a relatively recent time, and, like all Western histories of the nineteenth century, it's a blend of unbelievable innovation and uncomfortable colonization. The only reason I pulled the bio off the shelf and brought it upstairs was that I knew Cook's name. An old boss of mine was obsessed with Cook, along with Hemingway, steamer trunks, and anything tweed. This boss—a willowy Gwyneth Paltrow type who looked glamorous even in the safari-style khaki skirts, snakeskin belts, and clacking wooden bracelets she wore around Manhattan—ran a luxury travel company, where I was a copywriter, and she talked about travel elegiacally, the way literary critics discuss the death of the novel. "The Golden Age of Travel," she said more than once, "begins and ends with Cook."

Plenty of people living in the nineteenth century would have disagreed. Cook's tours caught on quickly, filling popular destinations with tourists and spawning imitators who did the same. Within two decades, Cook's tourists were everywhere and, if you listened to the critics, ruining everything.

Many critics were just snobs: the wealthy English in Egypt classed tourists among the plagues, sniggering at their gauche "wideawakes and tweeds" (the Hawaiian shirt and Bermuda shorts of the nineteenth century). Detractors also found fault with tourists' lack of "reason" for traveling. Not explorers traveling for discovery, merchants for gain, or aristocrats on educational or health pretexts,

Cook's clients toured for "the experience of strangeness and novelty," in the words of the sociologist Erik Cohen, "valued for their *own sake*." The italics are Cohen's, emphasizing how strange this was. It's still pretty strange, if you think about it, but now it's such a part of our culture— novelty is the primary theme of advertising, the raison d'être for the entertainment industry—that it's easy to overlook.

But the most common and lasting criticism was that tourists were changing the landscape. Hotels, a new invention, suddenly began to pop up everywhere, like "a white leprosy," according to the art critic John Ruskin, who took the tourist occupation of Switzerland particularly hard. Another one of Cook's peers complained that tours brought "cardinal British institutions—tea, tubs, sanitary appliances, lawn tennis and churches" to all corners of the globe. *The Sunday Review* fretted that rising numbers of tourists made true escape impossible: "We talk glibly enough of leaving England, but England is by no means an easy country to leave."

Tourism, when looked at this way, becomes an insidious form of colonization: instead of using military force and laws, tourists colonized with their pocketbooks and their habits.

Though Cook's mission was helping people kick "old corrupt customs," by "customs" he meant booze, and he was happy to oblige more innocuous requests, such as teatime. Businesses in tour destinations quickly followed suit; collectively, tourists were great for the economy of wherever they visited. Nearly two hundred years later, you can go almost anywhere in the world—from Taiwan to Equatorial Guinea—and stay in a Western-style room, eat Western-style food, start the day with coffee or tea and close it with a cocktail. The tourism economy is as much about catering to habits as it is about supplying novelty.

What seems on the surface like a positive transaction—tourists get hot beverages, locals get money—has been a source of contention ever since. Today, many travelers complain about the tourist economy for the same reasons they did in Cook's day. "Touristy" has become a derogatory term, describing places that attract tourists by catering to their habits, and every year more places gain this descriptor. As suggested by the *Wired* study of the most common phrases in successful dating profiles, the majority of us are attracted to the idea of exploring and trying new things; but the more people who trek out to find novel places, the less novel these places become. Pictures are posted online; people who see the pictures make plans to visit the new hot spots, where familiar foods and drinks and languages begin to appear, attracting even more familiar faces; and all this familiarity feels like the antithesis of adventure, reminding travelers of the mundane ordinary that they're trying to take a break from. Meanwhile, according to the author and Antigua native Jamaica Kincaid, locals who can't afford to travel often hate tourists for reasons that are "not hard to explain . . . they envy your ability to leave your own banality and boredom, they envy your ability to turn their own banality and boredom into a source of pleasure for

yourself." Feeling bored doesn't require any sort of privi-
lege, but doing something about it often does. Taking a
trip, seeing a movie, drinking a beer, wearing or eating
anything new and different all cost money.

Yet boredom doesn't necessarily go away when you're
doing any of these things, even traveling. Wherever we
are, time demands to be dealt with, and when managing
time—especially free time—habits are our handiest tool.
According to Camus, "everyone is bored, and devotes
himself to cultivating habits." Far from home, each day
lying unbroken before us, we might be forgiven for wanting to bookend that unwieldy stretch of time with a coffee at daybreak, a beer at dusk, and, for Cook's English
tourists, a cup of tea in the afternoon: habits that break
time into manageable chunks, even as they change the
places we visit.

Our dependence on habit and desire for novelty are both
so ingrained that usually we don't think about them.
While reading about them I *had* to think about them and
became annoyed with the coffee I was drinking, a symbol
of my reliance on habits—with a hot coffee I can sit still a
good half hour longer than usual—and my craving for
novelty, since it was a really unhealthy hazelnut cream
thing that I'd bought hoping the treat-like aura of it would
help me focus even better.

"Do you have the time?" the old man asked. His own
habitual beverage appeared to be untouched.

"Sure. Um, quarter past eleven," I told him, refraining from asking what I always want to ask: *Is it hard to read all day every day with an eye patch? Do you ever wish you had a different hobby?* At least I assume his library lurking is a hobby, but maybe it's work. That's why I lurk here. Or maybe he lives here, which would explain why he has no sense of time, as there aren't windows in the stacks. Watching him, I thought I might write (or at least be willing to watch) a TV show called *Stack Pirates*. Here's the scenario: a group of recent graduates can't find jobs (probably there's a recession), so individually they begin to spend their days in their college library in order to avoid roommates or landlords or parents, as well as the restless torpor of sitting around the house all day. Eventually they find one another and decide to band together and figure out how to live in the library full-time. Their guide on this quest is the old man with the eye patch, who they discover has been living in the library since his own graduation in the sixties (he was avoiding the draft, maybe). They call him the Captain, because of his eye patch but also because he's been obsessively researching the history of piracy for years, his own version of Ahab's white whale. I'm not sure what they do once he teaches them how to find food and where to sleep. Probably they solve crimes.

I realized I was staring and that my coffee, now that I'd spent so much time thinking about it, wasn't helping me focus anymore. I got up, stretched, and headed back down to the travel section. I pressed the elevator button a few times, but it seemed to stop on every floor, and after a few minutes I was so restless that I just took the stairs.

Modern tourism started in England, which makes sense—a colonizing country is probably a restless country—but by the mid twentieth century people from all over the world were touring. Tourism became a *thing*; you could tell because people had started studying it. The stacks are full of their books: *The Ethics of Sightseeing*, *The Language of Tourism*, *The Tourist Gaze*, and so on for longer than you'd care to read. Before venturing into the stacks I'd never read a book on tourism, but I knew the industry from working in it, first as a guide and then as a copywriter.

Like many people who grew up in small, gray-skied working-class towns (Cook, D. H. Lawrence, Geoff Dyer, to name a few), I'd always wanted to travel. It was the most obvious means of escape possible, and seemed like the cure for everything: small town, small life, sad family. My mom was a nurse, my dad a pastor, and both were depressed, which seemed at odds with their caregiving jobs. I was told that helping others gave purpose to life, yet the people who taught me this suffered painfully from a sickness defined by meaninglessness. He talked around the edges of suicide. She withdrew. I planned to get away.

But I couldn't just *go*. Unlike in most of the travel books I read and loved, in life there were practicalities to consider. I needed contact lenses and birth control. I needed to pay back my student loans. I needed cash. So—again, like Cook—I became a tour guide.

Unfortunately, I didn't really understand until I was one that most guides don't travel outside their "zone of expertise." Mine was first Alaska, then San Diego, and in each my adventures were limited to a square mile of sea on which I paddled a kayak while telling middle-aged tourists fun facts: leopard sharks aren't aggressive; sea lions *are* aggressive; the garibaldi is the state fish of California; an eagle's nest can weigh up to two thousand pounds.

As a copywriter I traveled more, but it was definitely business travel, which I actually prefer. Having to work gave my days structure and lent a purpose to sightseeing: if I was doing stuff in order to write about it, the purpose was work; if I was doing something unrelated, the purpose was shirking work. I find distractions most enjoyable when work is an obstacle.

Still, I wouldn't recommend copywriting to an aspiring traveler, at least not one who's as easily broken as I am. Writing marketing materials for tourism was like being asked to build a part for the mechanical innards of a beloved dog I'd always assumed, until being handed the screwdriver, was flesh and blood. According to my boss— the Paltrow ringer who loved Cook—true adventure was a thing of the past, which meant my task was to transform our travel company into a time machine, filling brochures with phrases like "timeless wilderness," "authentic villages," "hark back to the days of yore," "step into the past," "follow in the footsteps of explorers."

My boss wasn't nuts; she was practical. What I was doing in my midtown cubicle was the same as what any other travel copywriter was doing in any other cubicle.

Almost all travel advertising focuses on time: space tourism ads promise a glimpse of the future, tours for new parents or honeymooners offer the opportunity to press pause on the present ("time stands still," "live in eternal time"), but most often—so often that the sociologist Graham Dann accuses the industry of "unashamed wallowing in the past"—travel ads suggest that a certain tour, cruise, or even whole continent has the power to take us back in time.

The "past" of marketing is fictional. Sitting at my desk, whispering "adventure-scuffed decadence" at a computer screen, I created a whole world: the past in all its everything-is-fresh glory, sans poverty and oppression, plus modern plumbing, simultaneously ripe with novelty and fragrant with nostalgia. My everyday life paled in comparison. How could it not?

A fictionalized past is the most tempting of destinations. Even as far back as the sixteenth century, Don Quixote found life dull compared with the semi-mythical past of the novels he read. He loved the past so much more than the present that he began hallucinating that he actually lived there. Today, tour companies would love to replicate his madness. Even the most prosaic trip to my hometown could be an adventure if I saw the pimply motel desk guy as a castle keep and the town's Hummer factory as a training ground for battle-ready giants.

Granted, certain landscapes lend themselves to this brand of fantasy more than others. Travelers flooded New Zealand in record numbers after the *Lord of the Rings* movies were shot there. Ireland and Iceland similarly both received much-needed economic boosts from tourists who'd seen them in *Game of Thrones*. Cambodia's Angkor temples are hundreds of years older than Hollywood, but when I stood in Ta Prohm, a temple held in the grasping fingers of enormous tree roots, my first thought was not of the people who prayed there but of Indiana Jones. Entertainment has layered new meaning onto these old places, but they were chosen as shooting locations because they invited fantasy to begin with.

Cook's tourists were drawn to similarly past-evoking destinations. "The mystery of ages," he wrote in a promotional pamphlet, "is plucked from the vivid story of past centuries for those who thus sail in foreign seas and become familiar with many lands." He took his clients to Roman ruins, Egyptian pyramids, and Civil War battlegrounds (though actually, the last of these weren't historic quite yet, as tourists wrote home to report "skulls, arms, legs, etc., all bleaching in the sun"—war zones aren't always exciting for soldiers, as evidenced by the writing of Brian Turner and Shani Boianjiu, but war zones both ancient and fresh have long been fascinating to civilians in the same way that war stories are; companies specializing in "conflict tourism" offer tours of grave sites, concentration camps, and battlefields).

From Cook's brochures to mine, travel marketing seems to be to blame for our collective time-travel fantasy. But while ads certainly aggravate the situation, they're only responding to existing longings, the same as those of Don

Quixote: the desire to visit a world that's brighter and bigger than our everyday, never boring, and unblemished by anything as ordinary as habits.

To see this desire spelled out, I only had to look as far as the classics my boss encouraged me to read: Isak Dinesen on Africa, Bruce Chatwin on Patagonia, Henry Miller on Greece, D. H. Lawrence on Mexico—great sources for copywriters because they're all about escaping the bland present on a quest for an idyllic past. "We do not travel in order to go from one hotel to another, and see a few sideshows," wrote D. H. Lawrence. "We travel, perhaps, with a secret and absurd hope of setting foot on the Hesperides, of running up a little creek and landing in the Garden of Eden."

Tourism research, as it turns out, is built of the same behind-the-curtain stuff as copywriting, only more so. On the travel-section shelves are books on sex tourism, conflict tourism, health tourism, and party tourism (I suspect Cook would have appreciated that the last of these ended up being the bleakest, what with drunk spring breakers so regularly falling off balconies). Tourism's colonial undertones and emotional consequences were explored in depth. I learned about a condition called dromomania, whose sufferers have to be always on the move. Other people become so overwhelmed by the inconsistencies between travel marketing and real destinations that they become paranoid and delusional, a condition known as Paris syndrome for the frequency with which it happens to tourists visiting the famously romantic city. I learned about post-tourism, which is just research jargon for traveling hipsters: believing there's no authenticity left in the world, they enjoy tourist attractions ironically.

Sitting on the library floor between shelves, I paged through these books and traveled to some pretty dark places. When the timed lights between the shelves flicked off, it seemed appropriate.

What can get lost in all this research is that travel is a treat: the vast majority of our ancestors didn't travel for fun, and plenty of people now don't either. It's not free or mandatory. Like many other things we analyze and criticize—television, movies, books, foods, sports, social media, spas, and manicures—we always have the option to just opt out.

But, barring suicide, we can't opt out of life, so we've invented pastimes. Tourism interests me because it's not just a means to fill free time; by removing familiar places and faces and responsibilities, it makes free time *more* free.

There are different ways to deal with this. The kind of tourists who went on my kayak trips usually had lunch plans at an iconic restaurant afterward, then they'd visit a museum and/or ruin, then dinner and dancing. They'd straitjacketed their time with sightseeing. On the opposite end of the spectrum were clients of my Cook-loving boss's luxury travel company. In the brochures I wrote, travelers were encouraged to relish breakfast in bed and take luxurious afternoon siestas beneath gently swaying trees. This was their free time, and they were encouraged to answer Nietzsche's question "Free for what?" with "Naps!"

Between those two jobs, I had the chance to figure out what *I* would do with the freest of free time. After a couple of years of guiding, supplemented by working in restaurants, I'd saved enough to travel. A friend and I quit our jobs, sold our furniture, collected our security deposits, and left. We'd be backpackers, a lifestyle that sounded promisingly like that of travelers in books: we'd carry our lives in packs, eat street food, *not* take tours, meet locals, just . . . be free. We planned to travel this way for a month or two, until money got low, then come back to the United States and get new jobs (this would be harder than we'd hoped; I'd spend months cobbling together work before being hired by the Cook-loving boss). It was a reckless and exhilarating thing to do, or so we thought, until we stood in the middle of Khao San Road and realized that everyone else our age, from all over the planet, was doing the exact same thing.

We were officially on the Banana Pancake Trail.

Named for a dish commonly offered in anticipation of semibroke young Western tourists, the Banana Pancake Trail includes all the recommended destinations in the Southeast Asia edition of *Lonely Planet*. If you rely on that guidebook, as we did, then you're on the trail, and if you're on the trail, travel becomes less like an uncharted adventure and more like a stroll through the parking lot outside a Phish show. Dirty feet, tangled hair, fisherman's pants, and yoga beads adorned the bodies of our fellow travelers.

Beer, coffee, pancakes, cheap jewelry, and T-shirts printed with the region's unofficial motto—"Same-same but different"—were for sale in every town, giving meaning to the motto while giving us all familiar things to do: get caffeinated, bargain shop, eat, get drunk. Though we meant to have big adventures—like Don Quixote without the delusions—my friend and I turned out to be bigger creatures of habit than we had anticipated. We filled our free time with iced coffees and silver bangles.

"Same-same but different" described more than the trappings of tourism; it also described the experience of seeing other travelers over and over again. We ran into the same white-blond Australian in three different countries, an occurrence he assured us was "cosmic."

The Australian indulged in the same habits as we did, but without our "are we using this time right?" anxiety. He had no reason to be anxious; he was traveling indefinitely. Over the course of our first month, we'd met a surprising number of these "career travelers," people who didn't plan to return home soon or maybe ever. None claimed to be wealthy, but none were really poor either; they were all somewhere on the broad spectrum of middle-class. The Australian was the son of a plumber, and though he ardently did *not* like his father (most of the career travelers we met had bad relationships with their parents), it was from his father that he'd learned the skills that kept him on the road. Starting out working for room and board on a farm in Italy, he'd been so helpful that it led to a handyman job at a yoga retreat in India, which he'd parlayed into a landscaping position at a sister retreat in

Thailand, which he'd just quit when we met him. I learned all this at our second meeting, on an island in the Mekong, where a group of us tourists drank lukewarm beer and moved from the shade of one palm to another in an attempt to escape the midday heat.

"I've just always had this ability to know when it's time to move on," he told us. "I feel restless, you know? My mom's psychic so, I don't know, I probably inherited it."

You don't need to be psychic, I thought, to get bored. It was an uncharitable thought, but that afternoon I was irritated. Irritated with the sticky heat, with the strands of hair that stuck to my temples, with myself for having spent everything on this trip (was this how freedom was really meant to be used?), and again with myself for being irritable on the trip I'd spent all my money on (irritation was surely not the best way to use free time). All this irritation found its target in the unreasonably blond Australian who was always on the move.

"Cool," I mumbled. "Good for you." Then I excused myself to go swimming. After fighting the current for half an hour I was able to admit to myself that I didn't really think there was anything wrong with the Australian (besides the New Agey cosmic/psychic stuff). If you don't have kids and feel okay about not being insured, why not be transient? That's how past travel writers lived—Henry Miller, Patrick Fermor, Bruce Chatwin—and I like to think I could live like that too, but I don't, which was probably why the Australian irritated me. His life was more interesting than mine *and* he wouldn't stop talking about it.

Irritability is one of the key emotions psychologists associate with boredom. We get irritated standing in line, sitting in traffic, or listening to a long-winded story ("Every hero," wrote Ralph Waldo Emerson, "becomes a bore at last"). Our tendency toward bored irritation is why elevators have door-close buttons and crosswalks have request-to-walk buttons, even though most of those buttons don't actually do anything: pressing a button lets us believe that we have agency over our time. Maybe the Australian really knew how to be free, a secret that eluded me, or maybe moving was his version of a door-close button, allowing him to think he was changing because his surroundings changed, even though he brought his habits and hang-ups (the bad dad, the psychic mom) wherever he went. Maybe we weren't so different from each other.

"Excuse me, do you have the time?" asked the old man in the library.

"Let's see . . . half past four."

"Thank you," he said, which is what he always says, never "I'm late!" or even "Lunchtime!" He doesn't have anywhere else to be, as far as I can tell. He just likes to know.

What would I do if I had nowhere to be? Because I've been fortunate enough to travel aimlessly for a couple of months, I can tell you: I'd be irritable. Free time is daunting.

The world has been shaped by our inability to deal with free time. Cook intended for tourism to pull us out of the mundane ordinary, and people who can't travel (like Jamaica Kincaid's tourist-hating locals) desire to do so for that reason. We travel to escape a losing battle with time—the autoworker Ben Hamper's "war with that suffocating minute hand"—but we still have to deal with time, by napping it away or filling it with sightseeing or traveling to the brighter past that travel ads promise. For the majority of us, free time has proved too unwieldy to manage without habits, and, from Ruskin's "white leprosy" of hotels to the Banana Pancake Trail, the habits of travelers have reshaped the world.

It would be easy to admit defeat, to become the "post-tourists" researchers write about, committed to the idea that there's no such thing as authentic experience so we might as well laugh at it all. That seems like the most boring fate of all. Surely it's better to struggle, to scrimp and save, to be irritable swimming in the Mekong, and suddenly find yourself at a tiny empty beach surrounded by jungle where—if only for a minute or an hour or an afternoon, who can say—you escape time completely?

We might as well, because most of us will struggle either way. The parishioners who came to my dad for advice all asked versions of the same question: How can I be free? Free from grief, from anxiety, from anger. Free from the purposelessness of boredom, the result of a dull job or a stale marriage or the tedium of too many identical days in a small town. But, depressed, my dad wasn't free either; so there they sat, week after week, year after year, prisoners theorizing about their chains. Travel, at least in the books I read, offered to press pause on those questions in order to ask a single question that, if it could be answered, would make it one hundred times easier to figure everything else out: *Free for what?*

I still can't answer this question, and I haven't traveled much since I left the industry, unless you count voyaging restlessly, like the Australian, from floor to floor of the library stacks. Here's the sixteenth century, there's the twenty-third, and here's the Arctic, mis-shelved next to New Jersey. It's adventure of a sort, though you have to squint to appreciate it, like Don Quixote maybe, or my one-eyed companion, the original Stack Pirate, lost in his books, asking the time out of habit while I sip this hazelnut cream coffee for the same reason.

5

DRUNK WITH HAROLD HILL

My grandma's house was where I learned the phrase "The idle brain is the devil's playground," not from my grandma herself but from *The Music Man*, one of the six VHS tapes she owned, which my sister and I watched over and over to while away the time as the adults talked. Unstructured time like ours was dangerous, warned Harold Hill, the titular Music Man, in the form of a song sung to the concerned parents of River City. From playing pool on a sleepy afternoon it was a slippery slope to drinking and smoking, to gambling on horses and staying up all night with loose women (though Hill never actually says the words "slippery slope," maybe because *The Music Man* is set in 1912 and whoever was in charge of historical accuracy flipped through the *OED* and found that the use of "slippery slope" in phrases such as "he is on the slippery slope toward a life of crime" dates only as far back as 1951, the same year the United States passed the Boggs Act to levy maximum criminal penalties on drug smugglers).

"Trouble!" my sister and I chanted along with Hill, "with a capital T and that rhymes with P and that stands for POOL!"

The "idle brain" line wasn't nearly as catchy, but it stayed with me enough that it came back to me at a sleepover when I was a preteen and we watched *Idle Hands*, a movie about a lazy stoner whose hand goes on an independent killing spree. *Trouble, with a capital T* . . . Recently the line came back to me yet again, as if activated by a switch, during a very dull day working the polls for a local judgeship election. I'd bought a pick-four lottery ticket at the corner bodega over my lunch break, and the world-weary cashier who slowly punched my numbers into the machine used the time while I waited to warn me that playing the lottery "leads to trouble."

Everybody else working the polls had bought lottery tickets too; it was all we'd been talking about over the course of a long, slow day spent defending democracy for nobody in a high school cafeteria without cell service. "It's a nice way to pass the time, having a dream," one of my fellow workers had said, and I thought about repeating this to the cashier but instead opted for the more prosaic. "That's okay, thanks. I really only play it when I'm bored."

"Even worse," he said, shaking his head with disgust. Then, as if nothing had happened, no judgments made or fates decreed, he tore my ticket off the machine and passed it across the counter with an impassive "Good luck. Next?"

I didn't take it too hard. I should have known better than to mention I was bored. I've met so many people who are infuriated by the very word. They hear it as laziness, indifference, or entitlement—and sometimes it *is* used to mean those things. "Bored" is a big umbrella we use to cover a range of emotions; apathy huddled in close with irritability, restlessness, futility, loneliness, and despair.

Anyway, I had bigger problems than a cashier judging my purchases. I had trouble, *with a capital T and that rhymes with P . . .* —one of the world's catchiest songs lodged in my head for who knew how long. Like boredom, it was an affliction, and a particularly silly one. "I say your young men'll be fritterin'," I mutter-sang in the staccato cadence of Harold Hill as I walked back to the high school, back to an afternoon filled with talk about what we would do with our lottery winnings. "Fritterin' away their noontime, suppertime, choretime too."

Hill's warning was an old one, dating back all the way to the Old Testament: Proverbs in the King James Version of the Bible tells us that a good wife and mother "eateth not the bread of idleness," and King Solomon, the alleged author of Ecclesiastes, uses shoddy home maintenance as an analogy for human character: "By much slothfulness the building decayeth; and through idleness of the hands the house droppeth through." Presumably the lat-

ter is what Chaucer had in mind when he had the wife of
the titular character in "The Tale of Melibee" caution her
husband, "Solomon says that 'Idleness teaches a man to
do many evils'"—the precursor to "the idle brain is the
devil's playground." Rooted in religion, the notion is now
a topic of secular concern, heightened anew every June
when schools let out and news outlets print a slate of cau-
tionary headlines such as "Summertime Boredom Can
Lead to Uptick in Drugs, Alcohol Use for Kids."

I guess the idea is that if you're working you won't
have time to indulge in vices, but work doesn't necessarily squelch the desire. Dull work can even increase the
urge to transgress, like when I read "The Tale of Melibee"
and discovered, with help from frequent and necessary
Internet breaks, that the story is famously boring, with its
page after page detailing an aphorism-stuffed lecture from
Melibee's wife, Prudence. It's so boring that some schol-
ars have suggested that Chaucer wrote it as a joke, a sort
of meta-commentary on the failures of moralizing. While
I read I fantasized about better stories with more interesting characters. Harold Hill, for example—he moralized
plenty, but he also sang and danced and was secretly a con
man the whole time, fooling the people of River City into
thinking that he cared whether their kids turned into lazy
degenerates, when really all he wanted was to take their
money and flirt with the hot town librarian. "The Tale of
Melibee" would be vastly improved if it turned out that
Prudence was also a con artist, her minions robbing Melibee blind while she disabled him with her incredible
ability to bore. I checked the time on my phone for the

fourth time in, it turned out, as many minutes, and decided that this would all go down easier with a drink. I ran to the closest bodega and bought a tallboy in a paper bag to drink under the trees in the park while I finished "The Tale of Melibee," indulging in vice not for lack of anything else to do, but to sweeten the experience of doing something I wasn't psyched about.

"Drinking," in the words of Charles Bukowski, "joggles you out of the standardism of everyday life, out of every-thing being the same." I know a teacher who drinks wine while she grades papers, a social worker who smokes pot while he fills out end-of-day paperwork, a program-mer who likes to have a beer while checking code. Many of us work through happy hour but still celebrate it, with some even bringing computers to the bar. Imbibing on the job is a collective habit that could be blamed on our milieu as New Yorkers, our rents as high as our job market is competitive. Sometimes we're bored, but we're rarely idle, having left that behind in our grandmas' living rooms, when we'd watch musicals to drown out the deadly dull sound of grown-ups talking about stuff we'd probably have to worry about someday, but not yet.

This sort of carefree childhood idleness comes up often when I ask successful older adults about boredom. Child-hood boredom—uncomplicated by fears about whether the right choices were made, the right people loved—is easier to talk about than adult boredom. Most of the memories people share with me are fond, appreciative of how well a dull childhood fits into a narrative arc: "All those after-noons spent kicking the legs of our awful horsehair couch really motivated me to get out of that town and move to New York City. Now I'm a furniture designer!"

We talk about idle adults in very different terms. Free-loaders. Vagrants. Slackers. A grown-up Kerouac crashing at his mom's house and Bartleby the scrivener refusing to do any work because he "would prefer not to." They're heroes to some, wastes of space to others, but everyone tends to agree that, whether or not they use their free time to drink, smoke, steal, or gamble, they're transgressing already just by not working. "There's this notion that doing nothing represents this bohemian freedom," the ethnographer Martin Demant Frederiksen told me. "We talk about the joy of doing nothing while at the same time knowing it as something that undermines every value we have."

I got to know Frederiksen through his book *Young Men, Time, and Boredom in the Republic of Georgia*, which is much more engrossing than "The Tale of Melibee," even though the Georgians he interviewed kept telling him how terrible it would be. "This place is not very interesting," a Georgian waitress named Maya pointed out. "No one would ever read a book about young people in Batumi. I definitely wouldn't!" Unemployment was high, emigration was difficult, and there was a general feeling of "lack of possibility." Some dabbled in crime, while others coped, when they could afford it, with illegally obtained prescription pills and alcohol. Home to so much idleness, Georgia had surpassed being the devil's playground; the young men whom Frederiksen ended up focusing his study on called it "the devil's asshole." Despite, or because of, the Georgians' protests against their own appeal, Frederiksen told me that the hardest part about writing the book was that he "didn't want to make it seem too interesting."

"I've never heard a writer say that before," I told him. Being interesting was the primary concern in writing workshops I attended in college, so much so that when a student once told our class that she was a recovering heroin addict, the professor's first reaction was to assure her that she was dealing with "*great* material," and the one guy whose stories were always about misunderstood men drinking in jazz clubs grumbled an audible "*Lucky.*"

But that kind of thinking missed the point of his project, Frederiksen explained. Doing nothing wasn't a bohemian adventure for the men he interviewed in Georgia, nor was it a taste of freedom for him, an expat from Denmark, to be drinking vodka with the locals. "It was just horrible," he said. "Not because of them, understand, but the place. After three months I was physically bored. I had entire days where I barely got out of bed. I'd hear my phone ringing and not know whether to answer. And I realized: this is what's going on for these guys." As if to remind the reader that compelling narrative arcs are full of things nobody actually wants to live through, Frederiksen included the detail that a musician named Gosha would sometimes refuse to be interviewed as if he were in the present, preferring to pretend they were in the future looking back and laughing about how boring life was back then.

Talking with Frederiksen about how horrible this kind of boredom is helped make sense of one of the more confusing aspects of idleness: that we blame it for tempting people into vice, but also use it to punish people for giving in to vice. For months I'd been collecting news items about people who'd been arrested because of something they'd claimed to have done out of boredom, including a septuagenarian shoplifter in Britain, a Dutch supermarket employee who hacked into his company's corporate laptops, a group of housewives in China who started an underground gambling den, and a Canadian who smashed newsroom windows and explained his actions to the police by arguing that "poor people need to have fun too." They'd all broken laws because they had too much time on their hands, yet the biggest punishment they faced was prison, where they would have nothing *but* time on their hands.

How you can spend that time depends on what prison you're in. Most prisons in the United States have an outdoor track and television; some have gyms, libraries, and computers. A 2015 British prison inspection found that "boredom leads to violence" and suggested that prisons in the U.K. should offer more planned activities to curb fighting. In solitary confinement cells—colloquially known as the SHU, for "special housing units"—there isn't much to do at all. Billy Blake, who's been in the SHU since 1987, hasn't seen a TV since the eighties, has never been online or held a cell phone, and hasn't been outdoors in four years. "What you call boredom would seem a whirlwind of activity to me," Blake wrote in an essay for the advocacy group Solitary Watch. "I've . . . felt boredom and loneliness to such a degree that it seemed to be a physical thing inside so thick it felt like it was choking me, trying to squeeze the sanity from my mind, the spirit from my soul, and the life from my body."

Solitary confinement takes full advantage of the fact that loneliness and boredom often go together, blending so effortlessly that the poet Mary Ruefle sees them as essentially the same: "my definition of loneliness—to bore oneself." Boredom compounds loneliness, or maybe it's vice versa, but either way it's two tortures for the effort of one. And it really *is* torture, at least by the standards of Guantánamo, which included solitary confinement with beatings, sleep deprivation, and chaining prisoners in "stress positions" on its list of ways to grill suspected terrorists. Mohamedou Ould Slahi wrote *Guantánamo Diary* from solitary, writing it out by hand in the "small, free-standing prison hut" that he lived in for more than a decade.

Neither Blake nor Slahi was in solitary because of something done out of boredom, and the vast majority of people from the articles I'd been collecting had no chance of ending up in their shoes. With the notable exception of thrill kills, those who claim to have committed a crime out of boredom usually haven't done anything major. It's shoplifting and vandalism, illegal porn downloads and hacking, and drug-and-alcohol-related misdemeanors as far as the eye can see, impulses acted on just to take the edge off. Having received a twenty-five-dollar fine for public consumption while struggling through "The Tale of Melibee," I can relate.

The scope of the boredom-induced crime seems to depend on the degree to which the perpetrator experiences boredom—as Blake felt it in the SHU, or as Frederiksen observed it in the Georgians—as a painful lack of possibilities that must be physically escaped. In Algeria, for example, the boredom of village life is "unrelenting, unbelievable, unbearable and inhuman," according to the Algerian writer Kamel Daoud; emigration is punishable by up to six months in prison but the prisons are full to capacity with people who tried anyway. One man named Rachid has attempted escape three times. His situation isn't desperate, he told a reporter for the BBC. He has a menial job that pays the bills, but he says, "There's nothing for me here," and as a result of trying to leave and being sent back over and over he's become "so depressed."

Frederiksen's interviewees had also mentioned depression, or what they referred to as *dep'resia*, describing it as something they might succumb to if they were alone with their boredom for too long. The fact that they were vocally bored together helped keep them from falling into too deep a hole, even though being bored together also often meant getting drunk together—any need to stay out of trouble was outweighed by the need to be soothed by camaraderie. I appreciated this. I'd also been feeling easier in my skin since I'd started talking to people about boredom; it had gone from a project I avoided mentioning to something my friends and neighbors asked me about. There was less judgment than I'd expected, and a lot more solidarity than I'd anticipated, which helped me care less about the judgment that I *did* encounter, the "only boring people get bored" dismissal that didn't solve any problems but did, for a long time, make me silent about them. I wondered if this newfound openness about boredom would help me ward off depression, which runs in my family, the same way it helped the Georgians. What an immensely handy use of all this research that would be.

I knew boredom and depression were related, like boredom and loneliness. Erich Fromm has described boredom as "the average state of melancholia, whereas melancholia is the pathological state of boredom that one finds in certain individuals," which seems to imply that boredom is sort of like depression for the masses. But I didn't know what the actual neurological nuts and bolts of that relationship were, so I called a neuroscientist, James Danckert, who also happens to be one of the world's foremost boredom researchers.

Like most people who study boredom, Danckert also suffers from it, "and I use the word 'suffer' very deliberately," he explained, "because I really do find it an unbearable experience." A few years ago, he conducted a study with his fellow researcher John Eastwood to determine whether or not depression and boredom were distinct states, and they confirmed that, yes, while depression and boredom are highly correlated (meaning that people who experience one very often experience the other) and share many components, such as a perceived lack of life meaning, they are in fact distinct. "The primary difference," Danckert explained, "is that if I'm bored, I still have a key component that the depressed person doesn't have, which is motivation." The motivation to avoid boredom manifests itself in all sorts of activities, from sneaking a drink on a slow workday to writing an essay in solitary confinement. The choice of vice or virtue depends on the person—Sherlock Holmes chose both, avoiding tedium by doing cocaine *and* solving crimes. Vice is perhaps a more common choice than virtue, if only because boredom is such a powerful motivator that it can turn otherwise neutral activities *into* vices: according to a 2015 study, the average person checks his or her phone eighty-five times a day, prompting *ChicagoNow* to suggest that checking our smartphones is the new cigarette break.

Meanwhile, for depressed people, according to the writer Andrew Solomon, it's difficult just to find the motivation to put on socks.

Solomon is a depression expert in the way that Danckert is a boredom expert, having both suffered from it and studied it extensively in order to write *The Noonday Demon: An Atlas of Depression*. Solomon isn't a particularly religious guy, but the concept of the noonday demon, like that of the idle brain being the devil's playground, has roots in religion that stretch all the way back to the Desert Fathers. The theologian Michael Raposa defines the noonday demon as "a powerful boredom that 'besieges' the devotee." Solomon sees it as one of the earliest names for depression. It might just be a matter of semantics. "In June 1994, I began to be constantly bored," writes Solomon as he recounts his first major depressive episode.

I'd reached out to Solomon because Danckert had explained that, while both depression and boredom are preceded by an inability to engage, we don't know "what turns that failure into depression instead of boredom, or vice versa," or if boredom, left unchecked, might turn into depression, restlessness sliding into despair like the kids of River City drifting from a game or two of pool after school to all-night carousing with libertine women. I understood that by "we" Danckert meant science, which meant that no amount of spelunking in the archives would turn up anything definitive. This was fine because, as I'd learned from growing up with depressed parents who manifested the disease in two very different ways, depression is highly variable. For a long time I didn't know much more about it than that. Despite my having grown up around it, my understanding of depression is murky, based on two people who didn't like to talk about it. I believe now that they wanted to protect us from worrying about them, especially after our aunt committed suicide when my sister and I were in elementary school. They wanted, I believe, to assure us that we wouldn't lose them too, and the effect was that we didn't talk about mental illness in our home. Solomon, on the other hand, has spent many years of his life documenting his own depressions and perfecting ways to express how the disease has twisted and turned through his mind over the years.

He explained to me that boredom acts for him as a warning sign of impending depression. Over the course of several depressive episodes he's learned to differentiate between "the everyday, I'm-playing-with-my-kid-and-we've-built-everything-we-possibly-can-with-Legos kind of bore-dom," and an all-encompassing feeling that *everything* is boring: the work he cares about, the people he loves, the activist role he's come to play in many public conversa-tions about mental illness, politics, and LGBT issues. "That's when I know I have to watch out," he told me. "I get more exercise, more sleep, maybe talk to my therapist about changing my prescription dosage."

"And that works? I mean, you can stop yourself from getting depressed?"

"Not always, but often."

Solomon is lucky, he reminded me, lucky in the same way I am, just to have these yardsticks by which to mea-sure boredom. Statistically, most people don't have jobs they care about, and the "emphasis on finding identity and meaning through work can make people who aren't finding that feel like they're not as good," in the words of Dior Vargas, founder of the People of Color and Mental Illness Photo Project, who also told me that being unem-ployed triggered her own depression. Many of the Geor-gians whom Frederiksen interviewed didn't have jobs either, and would vie for work they knew they wouldn't care about. "Being bored over an extended period of time can be depressing in and of itself," said Solomon. "It's both a symptom and a cause."

I was lucky to spend my days with work I care about, even if the occasional task, such as reading "The Tale of Melibee," drove me crazy. I was doubly lucky that this meant I could follow Solomon's example: to daily make the effort not to conceal moments of boredom behind a wash of alcohol or a haze of smoke, or try to trick myself out of feeling it by seeking out a new landscape or a stranger's body, but to pay attention and learn to parse average tedium from the more important stuff, signs of depression or indications to move on. "Depression is the flaw in love," writes Solomon, and boredom is like a spill on love's fabric, something you can clean up if you're paying attention but that becomes a stain if left unnoticed and unnamed for too long.

It wasn't long before I had a chance to practice this technique. After working at the college all day on a Tuesday, I took the train up to Union Theological Seminary, entered one of the old brick-and-limestone buildings, and passed through the quiet courtyard and into the other side of the building, where room upon room full of books make up one of the largest theological collections in the country. I was there to get a book Solomon had mentioned, Kathleen Norris's *Acedia & Me*. It's another book about the noonday demon, but instead of defining it as boredom, like Michael Raposa, or depression, like Solomon, Norris calls it acedia—the same term that the Desert Fathers used—and treats it as a completely separate third thing, which she tracks through her life: as a child, as a poet, as the wife of a depressive alcoholic, as a widow and a writer.

It was a good story, but still I kept looking up and away, distracted by birdsong or the buzz of my phone or the whisper of turning pages. I was reading in the courtyard, sitting on a stone bench next to a man I assumed to be a student. One glance at him could break your heart, or at least my heart, that of the daughter of an often unhappy priest who was also once an eager seminary student. His head was bent over a cloth-bound Bible, his hair badly cut into a sort of bowl, his finger tracing the numbered lines at a bright pace, as if searching for something—the secret to finding meaning, maybe, or love or eternity. I understood the appeal. Regardless of how rarely you actually find any big life secrets in an old book, it always seems like that's where they'll be, if they're anywhere. The Bible was my first really old book, the mystical fascination of my churchgoing days presaging my trade as a researcher.

This was maybe why I was having a tough time with *Acedia & Me*. I hadn't been to church in years and had long assumed I was out for good, but religion kept pulling me back in, like the mob tugging at Michael Corleone. It snuck into my research on boredom in the form of the Desert Fathers, the devil's playground, and Ecclesiastes, which in the New International Version of the Bible opens with " 'Meaningless! Meaningless!' says the Teacher. 'Utterly meaningless! Everything is meaningless!' " and happens to be the favorite book of one of P. G. Wodehouse's most pessimistic housekeeper characters, Nannie Bruce. In Solomon's research on depression he also kept coming across religion, so often that he ended up naming his book after a medieval monks' affliction. Both depression and boredom were rooted in this medieval religious world that our Western culture had supposedly left behind, trading it in for a secular society that somehow still has the same problems.

I was weary of revisiting this old world; the same world where Norris had settled for good, after years away from religion, in part because she felt drawn to the idea of acedia. She defines it as a vice, noting that it was originally one of the deadly sins. This way of thinking apparently works for Norris, but I felt tired and sad just reading it, reminded of a long-ago night—I was maybe ten—when I woke my dad to tell him that I'd eaten the leftover pizza in the fridge and had a stomachache. Not fully awake, he mumbled, "Gluttony's a sin," and rolled over, unwittingly adding an anxiety twist to my preexisting stomachache. There's really no problem so awful, to paraphrase *Calvin and Hobbes*, that you can't make it worse with guilt.

6

A. J. LIEBLING IN A NAP POD

I googled Google before I visited Google, just to know what to expect. Also because I like googling things. I regularly google reviews of shows I like, pictures of old celebrities when they were young, life stories of dead authors, and articles about smart animals (octopuses are so smart that they're given puzzles so they won't get bored in captivity). As much time as I fritter away googling, I fritter even more away checking Gmail, even though I don't like reading or responding to e-mail. It's a weird thing everyone I know does—complain about e-mail and check it *all the time*. Gmail has only been around since 2004, as I learned from googling Google, and it's remarkable how much it's changed life since then. I read that the irregularity with which e-mail arrives is the pattern most likely to provoke addiction, which led me to a Thoreau quote: "In proportion as our inward life fails, we go more constantly and desperately to the post-office." Thoreau would have hated Gmail, but then he hated a lot of things. I think he would have had a harder time hating YouTube, another Google product, if only because the site has so many nature videos.

With all the sidetracks, diversions, and wiki wormholes, I spent more time googling Google than I planned to spend at Google proper. I was just going there to meet my friend Walker for lunch. He works there, but I don't know exactly what he does. When we talk about Google we talk only about the unlimited food, the gym, the free gadgets, and the game room.

"Do you want a coffee?" he asked when I arrived, entering through a pristine lobby with a big sign that read: "We're undergoing renovations, please excuse the mess."

"Aren't we going to lunch?"

"We are, I just meant for on the way," he answered. "I have to stop at my desk and there's a kitchen right there. You can make yourself a latte."

You can make yourself a latte every three hundred feet in Google. You can also make yourself a cocktail and a bowl of theater-quality popcorn, a snack that pairs nicely with a Netflix session in one of the nap pods. More than a couple of people were doing this at 12:30 on a Thursday afternoon. Never have I wanted to work at a tech company so badly.

"Yeah, it's great," agreed Walker. "But," he quickly demurred, "they'd probably pay us more if they didn't give us all this stuff. So, there's no free lunch, right?"

The saying lost some of its poignancy because I was about to eat a really incredible free lunch. The dessert bar was so fantastic that I went back twice. The only jarring note was a warning on a pan of strawberry-walnut pudding: "contains: beef and pork." "From the gelatin," explained a Google employee next to me, a short guy with dreadlocks wearing a T-shirt with a line of code printed on it, as if someone had told him to dress up like a Google employee.

The whole office was like that, so exactly what I expected that it felt staged. Everyone was young, and everyone was either racing around or aggressively relaxing. One room had a wall of drawers full of different-colored Legos facing another wall lined with Lego structures—houses, dinosaurs, double helixes—that employees had built. Another room was designed to look like an old-timey train station, with subway car conference rooms. There were massage chairs, pinball machines, and pool tables. People zipped past us on scooters or stood rapt behind standing desks, brows furrowed in enviable concentration. The only thing missing was a Ping-Pong table. "Too Facebook," said Walker, "but we do have an amazing video game collection."

"Hmm?" I had lost track of what he was saying as I stared at a woman lying back in one of a row of massage chairs, laughing out loud at a show on her phone. She was about my age, and I could picture myself in her place, my restless mind at peace, recharging for another bout of focused work. This version of me wouldn't work herself into an unrecognizable state, googling like a child on methamphetamines. She didn't need to google; she *was* Google. I choked on something, either a laugh or a sob. To clear my throat, I took another sip of Google latte, my second coffee in two hours. It was delicious.

Suffice it to say, things hadn't been going so well. It was the middle of the semester, I had multiple research clients, and work was piling up, my weekdays slowly blending with my weekends in one long, tepid slog; my only breaks not proper breaks at all, but frequent and unnecessary visits to Google or the *New York Times* webpage or my e-mail inbox, anything allowed by my productivity software (which blocks things like Netflix and Instagram with the passive-aggressive question "Shouldn't you be working?"). Reading the news and doing the *Times* mini crossword had the additional advantage of allowing me to half believe that I was broadening my perspective and exercising my mind instead of procrastinating, even though procrastinating was exactly what I was doing. Restlessness was causing me to waste time, even as it increased my anxiousness over the scarcity of time. It had gotten so bad that I'd actually visited a psychiatrist to see if I could get ADD medication, but after a consultation and a test he advised against it. "I don't recommend it for people with a history of anxiety," he explained. "Anyway, you don't need it. Your test scores were excellent." But he couldn't tell me why my perfect focus on the ADD test didn't translate to perfect focus at work. *I can't even pass an ADD test*, I thought; *I'm failing at* everything.

It didn't make sense—I feel lucky to have two great jobs, but still I'm restless and distracted. At least I'm not alone: a *Times* op-ed about this *exact problem* was side-barred with a long list of comments along the lines of "Clicking on 'Addicted to Distraction' as I try anything to avoid writing my paper . . ." and "As I was reading this very excellent article, I stopped at least half a dozen times to check my email." I read all the comments, as I increasingly did for most articles. I hadn't seen a movie or read a book in what felt like ages, but I somehow found the time to read hundreds of Internet comments written by strangers for "research." Mine was the strange half-life of the fad dieter, gorging on an entire loaf of tasteless gluten-free bread and congratulating myself on my virtuous abstinence.

But what could I do? I'd already read more than enough articles about digital detoxing. It's one of our perennial topics now, like parenting and healthy eating—just one more thing to collectively worry about. Baratunde Thurston wrote one of the earlier pieces on the subject, a 2013 cover story for *Fast Company*, and I called him up to ask his advice. Baratunde has been giving me advice since I first met him, back at *The Onion* in 2009, where he was director of digital and I was an editorial intern and he sat down with me to tell me everything I needed to know to be a freelance social media manager, which was how I paid my rent for three months between jobs. Social media is his forte; it's where he works and plays and spends so much time that he once had to quit the Internet just to get his life back, which is what he wrote about in the *Fast Company* cover story. "But I couldn't keep that going forever and function in the world," he told me. "Now I end up doing most of my creative work on the train. It's the only place where I don't have cell service."

Digital detoxing just didn't seem to get to the root of the problem. It was more complicated than that. Well before the coining of the term "digital detoxing" or the creation of the Internet as we know it, back in the eighties, the social critic Neil Postman warned that television had "made entertainment itself the natural format for the representation of all experience." If that sounds overdramatic, just chew on this sampling of news stories from 2015: President Obama urged religious leaders to write more entertaining sermons in order to compete with terrorist recruitment videos, the news anchor Brian Williams admitted that he out-and-out made things up in order to make his war stories more compelling, and MIT designed an algorithm to predict whether people will find a given photo interesting or boring. They're making it into an app to help us all be more fascinating for one another.

No wonder I'm so distracted. No wonder we all are. The problem isn't technology per se, but the expectations it has engendered: a steady stream of entertainment and stimulation. Or, as Bertrand Russell—who lived through the invention of electric lights, radio, and television—put it: "We are less bored than our ancestors were, but we are more afraid of boredom. We have come to know, or rather to believe, that boredom is not part of the natural lot of man."

The Google office, crammed as it was with games and toys and dessert bars for grown-ups, was an unlikely alternative. On the surface it seemed like just another part of the problem, and I knew, practically speaking, that Walker was right—there is no such thing as a free lunch, and even companies with game rooms and massage chairs don't always promote the perfect balance between work and leisure; odds were, at least some of those Google employees who appeared to be hard at work were actually looking at Facebook or watching Beyoncé videos. But I liked that there was an *ideal*, even if it didn't always pan out: the employees were expected to work hard at their standing desks, then relax hard, repairing to a game pod or massage chair—never fracturing their time and thus achieving Mihaly Csikszentmihalyi's concept of flow in both activities. There was something attractive and old-fashioned about this, reminiscent of A. J. Liebling, the mid-twentieth-century *New Yorker* writer, who apparently wrote so physically that he'd sweat through his shirt, occasionally laughing out loud at his own prose. Afterward, he'd go out for an outrageous meal, consuming at least two bottles of wine and several whole birds. I prefer movies to meat, but some combination of Google and Liebling would really be proper living. It was worth a try, anyway.

Walking into my apartment after visiting Google was like walking out of a movie theater at dusk. What had been normal now seemed flat and faded. There was re-search to be done, e-mails to respond to, but as a free-lancer I could feasibly do that all at night, so I unplugged my computer and carried it away from my tidy desk and over to the blanket-and-cushion-strewn couch, which would have to do for a nap pod. Then I disabled my pro-ductivity settings.

It does something to you, disabling your productivity settings. It's a real commitment to *not* being productive. There's a line drawn in the sand, a definitive decision that means you're absolutely not going to watch just one epi-sode of a show. I watched three episodes of *New Girl*, a sitcom about a bunch of zany, good-looking roommates who constantly pull pranks on one another. I don't know any real adults who pull pranks, with the exception of a guy who proposed to his girlfriend via a fake letter saying she was losing her insurance. He suggested she get on his insurance . . . by marrying him. She ended up married to someone else.

As badly as that went, it might not be terrible if we all pulled more pranks. Or crafted more puns, or made more time for general personal zaniness (though such plentiful time, judging by *New Girl* at least, might require frequent, albeit hilarious, unemployment). In 2015, MTV surveyed teenagers in twenty-six different countries and found that 97 percent of them are often bored, but the highest-rated "cure" for this feeling was humor. This made sense to me, as I pictured Liebling laughing at his desk, and it helps explain the preponderance of silliness on the Internet, from *Onion* headlines to hyperviral "funny cat" videos on

YouTube to *BuzzFeed* lists of the world's funniest texts, tweets, Tumblr posts . . . and on and on.

MTV executives admitted they were surprised by these results. They'd gone into the study assuming that teenagers today—so many of whom have constant contact with their friends via smartphones, plus access to all the varieties of entertainment the Internet has to offer—would never be bored. Instead they found that "mindlessly browsing the Internet" was rated *the* most boring activity teenagers engage in, more than school or work.

That word "mindlessly" bugged me when I first read it, and bugs me still, because it reminds me of its opposite, "mindfully," a term that smacks of sanctimonious yoga teachers and wellness gurus—anyone who implies that if you just follow their advice, you'll be happy. As if happiness were so simple, a pair of one-size-fits-all pajamas you can order online and snuggle up in for the rest of your days, swaddled in the polar fleece of meaningful existence.

Mindfulness advocates used to be the sort of people who, if they brought up boredom at all, would do so by posting that wildly popular Louis C.K. boredom meme on their Facebook walls, a picture of the comedian's face next to a quote from his TV show: " 'I'm bored' is a useless thing to say. I mean, you live in a great, big, vast world that you've seen none percent of. Even the inside of your own mind is endless; it goes on forever, inwardly, do you understand? The fact that you're alive is amazing, so you don't get to say 'I'm bored.' " This mentality—like that of anonymous Internet commenters telling refugees to "sod off back to where they came from" if they're bored in refugee camps—sees boredom purely as a failure of gratitude, when it deigns to see it at all.

Though Louis himself has countered this attitude plenty of times over the years, particularly in his jokes about bored masturbation, the attitude of most mindfulness advocates toward boredom didn't seem to shift until around 2015, when an episode of NPR's *Note to Self* podcast, "Bored and Brilliant," aired, focusing on the risks of constantly checking our smartphones. The host, Manoush Zomorodi, claimed she hadn't been bored since she got her first smartphone seven years before, and declared that this was a problem. She'd spoken to researchers, done the reading, and come to the conclusion that "we get our most original ideas when we stop the constant stimulation and let ourselves get bored."

For many people this is true, but it's just a facet of the truth about boredom. Unfortunately, edutainment tends to present complex stuff as really simple, which usually amounts to soft lying. News outlets picked up Zomorodi's nuanced report and produced a flurry of articles that dumbed it down, conflating boredom with mindfulness and unplugging, even as—*at the exact same time*—MTV was busy recalibrating its content and marketing strategy to appeal to a world full of teens who were bored because they were *too* plugged in, their boredom a product not of mindful abstinence from technology but of mindless scrolling and clicking.

None of this really has anything to do with *New Girl*, except for the fact that I read about it while watching

New Girl, because it turns out I'm as incapable of being entertained without working as I am of working without being entertained. I was hunched over my computer on the couch, lost in the forgoing-mindfulness/mindlessness whirlwind, no longer laughing at the high jinks of the characters, who were all half-hidden behind my googling window anyway.

I shouldn't have tried to relax with my computer. Computers and smartphones blur the line between work and entertainment, tool and toy. I use Microsoft Word to write and Google Chrome to check e-mail, watch TV, and read articles, but they're both on the same machine. My fingers touch the same keys regardless of what I'm accessing. The whole point of disabling my productivity settings was to try to separate entertainment from work, but—like my mom, who loved *Roseanne* but always felt guilty watching TV, so she only ever watched the show when there was laundry to fold—I had proven incapable of doing that, at least not on my computer, or by myself. Home entertainment in general makes me restless, which I attribute to the fact that I occasionally work from home. My desk in the bedroom is clearly visible from the living room couch, and when I try to relax it taunts me with its pot of pens and piles of scrawled-on Post-its and the billboard on the wall above it, full of quotes and cards from friends and to-do lists. That particular weekday afternoon was also too quiet, an eerie absence of sirens and construction noises rising from the street outside, and I felt my aloneness more than usual. The sun was starting to shine weakly through the rain and into the living room, urging me to seize the damn day—*You only get so many days*, my restlessness said, *don't waste them!* Probably the best thing was to get out of there completely. "Mothers of America," pleaded Frank O'Hara, "let your kids go to the movies!" And to the movies I went.

There's a movie theater right down the block from our apartment. Our neighborhood isn't known for its heavies, but I have seen a couple of fights break out at this theater, and they were all phone-related. Somebody checks their e-mail with the screen brightness up all the way, or they leave their ringer on and someone calls in the middle of an important scene, or—god forbid—they answer that call in the theater itself, and suddenly there's yelling, cursing, more yelling at the curser for cursing in a family theater, and so on. If I tried to do any work at this theater I'd probably end up in a screaming match. As an extra precaution, I left my phone at home.

It's a similar theater to the one that's the setting for Annie Baker's play *The Flick*: frayed seats, weird ceiling stains, sticky floors, disgruntled staff. The entirety of *The Flick* takes place in this grungy fictional theater, where employees talk or argue or sweep in communal silence. The play is three hours long. My boyfriend and I scored tickets on the last weekend of the run, and during intermission we overheard the middle-aged woman next to him complaining loudly about the length of the first act. She was visibly enraged, cheeks red, eyes bright, hands furiously zipping her coat up and down, up and down, until she finally settled on up and stormed out to brave the cold and the loss of half her ticket's cost. Later I found out that so many people had complained about *The Flick*'s length and lack of action that the theater owner had written an e-mail—sent to all the theater's subscribers and later published in *The New York Times*—explaining his reasons for running the play (which essentially amounted to, *it's good*, an opinion later seconded by the Pulitzer committee). The amazing thing about all of it was how *furious* so many people were. The play wasn't racist or homophobic, sexist or crude—all the things I normally associate with righteously angry responses. It was just sort of boring.

I had no beef with *The Flick*; it was really funny, which canceled out the boredom for me. But I experienced a fury similar to that of *Flick*-haters a few years ago, at a movie with my friend Rachel. It was an art movie, so I ought to have known better. So much modern art is deliberately monochrome, slow, or repetitive—even John Baldessari's declaration "I will not make any more boring art" is presented as a repeating line of text, over and over and over, *I will not make any more boring art, I will not make any more boring art, I will not make any more boring art* . . . more like a meta joke than a serious motto. Still, I wasn't prepared for how long and boring and ugly the art movie turned out to be. There was no color, no action, and absolutely no jokes. Instead I experienced something like a super-low-grade PTSD, a sort of post-dullness stress disorder, vividly reminded of years when I'd been stuck in ugly places, doing tedious work, with no money to sweeten my free time. Maybe this is why modern art is so often boring, and why boring entertainment makes people so angry: in a culture of constant stimulation and myriad distractions, that kind of stripped-down nothing-happening boredom can really be a shock to the system.

This enrages some people, but others like it, maybe even need it, and the entertainment industry has been taking note. In a strange reversal of Postman's theory that everything is now expected to be entertainment, entertainment outlets themselves have begun to offer fare such as the BBC's *Goes Slow*, a series of ultra-boring videos kicked off by a four-hour real-time canal boat journey. As constant action becomes the norm, traditionally boring fare seems different and interesting, in addition to offering the system-shocking benefit of boring entertainment.

In theory I understand these benefits: boredom forces us to pay attention, to slow down, to feel things. But in practice, I'd really rather be entertained. That's what entertainment is *for*, after all—it's in the *name*. This is especially true at the movies. The first rule of filmmaking, at least according to Billy Wilder, is "Thou shalt not bore."

So I bought a ticket to *Star Wars: The Force Awakens*— I'd already seen it, but it was the only movie in the place that promised not to be slow-paced and not to try to teach me something (beyond, I guess, don't be evil). The only other people in the lobby that Thursday afternoon were a smattering of gray-haired men and women, presumably retirees, and a small pack of teen boys with a collective elation that gave the impression they were blowing something off, afternoon homework or sports practice or whatever. A weekday matinee was so outside my normal routine that it felt like I was getting away with something, like I needed to hide, though I couldn't say from whom. I quickly ducked into the dark theater, a few rows behind the teens, and settled in for a bout of pure entertainment, lightsabers and all.

Because I'd already seen the movie, it was perhaps too easy to get distracted, especially since one of the teenage boys was giving a barely whispered lecture to his buddies on three-way sex. This might have been worrying if the boys weren't so obviously nerds, their knowledge so clearly derived from television and the Internet. "Look," whispered the ringleader, while Kylo Ren prayed to the twisted mask of his granddad Darth, "if you *gotta* do it with another dude, it's *gotta* be a friend, right?"

My mind drifted away from the action on-screen and onto an imagined Web series, *The Teen Commandments*. Each episode would just be this particular teen fervently delivering advice on one topic—which would be different episode by episode—to his crew in a darkened movie theater. The production budget would be next to nothing, not much more than the cost of the teens' tickets and popcorn, and the show would be educational. Sort of. "Here's the most important thing," I heard him whisper. He paused for effect, and the congregation leaned in to hear him better over the lightsabers. "You and the other guy, you gotta make eye contact, like, *the entire time.*"

I laughed out loud. Onscreen, bad guys were fighting good guys, blood was oozing from lightsaber wounds, and the future of the universe was dicey. The teens turned around as a unit, sized me up, and then sat forward as their ringleader—the acne-ridden Moses of *The Teen Commandments*—whispered, "Weirdo."

Training my eyes on the screen, pretending to be unaware of the teens, I tried not to blush. As a teenager I probably would have said the same about a grown-up alone at the movies on a weekday afternoon, and as an adult I wasn't so sure I would have been wrong. In the apartment by myself, I'd been able to half believe that I was one of the tech elite, curled up for a company-sanctioned Netflix session in a company-ordained "relaxation room" or attending a company-hosted movie lunch with free snacks (one of the regular events at King Entertainment, makers of *Candy Crush*). But the judgment of teen Moses was a reminder of the obvious: there was no company to host or sanction. There was just me: a weirdo and—now that I was thinking about companies and coworkers and group movies—a little lonely.

Those of us who experience restlessness are also likely to experience loneliness, researchers say—or rather, they say, "A high score on the Boredom Proneness Scale is highly correlated with a high score on the UCLA Loneliness Scale." Why UCLA got to claim loneliness, I don't know. Maybe because of the L.A. traffic, everyone isolated in their cars for hours every day, easing the tedium by calling or texting other people who are likewise alone in *their* cars. This is such a common fix to the loneliness and boredom of driving solo that a full quarter of American car accidents involve cell phones, according to government estimates. This is obviously terrible. Still, slouched low in my shabby theater seat, all I could think was that I regretted leaving my own phone at home. For all the things my smartphone offers—news apps, games, books, videos, weather, music, alarm, flashlight, notepad, crossword app—a quick and easy connection to the outside world will always be tops for me.

Still, as the credits rolled, the universe more or less safe for the time being, I decided *not* to go straight home—back to my phone and work and Wi-Fi—but to the most comforting place I know, incidentally also the mother ship for us weekday weirdos: the public library.

The sun was going down, a bitter wind was picking up, and the single large, overheated room that is my local public library was full of people taking shelter from the elements, and from unstructured time. It was the hour when such time weighs heaviest, what a stay-at-home mom I know calls the "witching hour" (because it's when her kids are most apt to act like they've been possessed by cranky demons) and what dozens of Craigslist personal ads simply refer to as afternoon boredom (as in: "w4m: Who is out there chillin and online? afternoon boredom strikes again . . ."). This was the time of day when my mom used to bring us to the library, after school for us and work for her, as the light died and a thin winter wind blew into town laden with the sour mash smell of the nearby ethanol plant. The library was pure pleasure for her, a source of entertainment that didn't make her feel guilty, unlike TV. Browsing the stacks buoyed her flagging five o'clock spirits, and she passed that on to me.

There are few places less like Google than my local library. Nobody moves fast, probably because most of them are old and because you can't drink lattes in the library. A sign on the door forbids drinks, along with food, skateboards, and loitering, the last of which is clearly a joke. The library *is* where you loiter, a haven for retirees and the unemployed—that's its twenty-first-century function. Well, that, and providing Internet. Something like sixty million Americans don't have Internet access, but every public library I've ever been in has had at least one table full of computers with slow Internet, free to use.

Per usual, the computer table at my library was fully occupied that winter afternoon, as were the tables nearby, unofficially designated for all the people waiting for computers. I nodded to the handful of people I see regularly, who seemed glad for the momentary distraction from leafing absently through books and sighing impatiently. Their troubles with boredom were different from mine. If they owned smartphones to while away the wait with, they wouldn't need to wait in the first place.

This made me think again of the "Bored and Brilliant" podcast episode, and the concept of digital detox in general. Plenty of people have too much stimulus, but others would frankly prefer to have more; or, as Baratunde put it when we talked about unplugging, "depending on your economic and social situation, boredom is either something you're running toward or running away from." Though we were talking about technology, there's nothing particularly modern about the idea of an economic schism in boredom. In the nineteenth century, the aristocratic Tolstoy described boredom as "a desire for desires," while the working-class Chekhov wrote about it primarily as a desire for escape.

Very few of our modern issues with distraction and restlessness are without precedent. Technology has made focus harder, but it's never been exactly *easy*. In his *Confessions*, St. Augustine berates himself for being distracted from prayer by the entertaining actions of spiders and crickets—the e-mail inboxes and *New York Times* articles of the fourth century. And Liebling . . . well, he isn't really an example of old-fashioned work habits, per se. He was an anomaly in his own time, which was why people bothered to document his habits in the first place. This is how history entertains, and how it misleads.

I drifted away from the computers, toward the books. In front of the "Fiction D–F" shelves, a man in his twenties or thirties was napping in a faded library chair, his chin tucked into his striped sweater, arms crossed high over his chest in the pose favored by macho men who want people to know they're only at this museum or art gallery or whatever under duress. He looked like someone from the past, some simple, uncomplicated, and purely fictitious age.

Fiction was where I belonged too, at least that afternoon. I sat down in a chair not far from the napping man, in front of "Fiction A–C." The wind was wailing around the building, and when I closed my eyes all the typing on the outdated computer keyboards could have been from a roomful of typewriters. I pulled a book off the shelf closest to me, one of Agatha Christie's Miss Marple stories, a problematic old favorite like most old favorites— really like most of history in general. The fictional past wasn't where I wanted to live; I just wanted to rest there for a minute, gathering my strength among old friends. I opened the book and began to read.

READING THE PHONE BOOK
IN AN INFINITELY EXPANDING
INFLATIONARY SEA

I'd only been studying boredom in earnest for a few months when Joelle called to tell me about a boredom event, "Something to do with creativity; it's a WNYC thing." WNYC is our local public radio station and their events nearly always sell out, attracting the many New Yorkers who listen to their podcasts while commuting. That they were actually hosting a boredom-themed event felt major: proof that I was researching something other people might care about.

It couldn't have come at a better time. I'd been spending my days blowing dust off library books, taking the elevator up and down between the Columbia stacks and the library café, overidentifying with the sad fourth-century monks I read about—among the first to recognize and document their own boredom—who prayed for hours alone in the desert and felt "such lassitude of body and craving for food, as one might feel after . . . hard toil."

Seasoned writers tell me this is all normal. They've even given me advice: keep books of poetry close at hand, work in timed increments, go for a walk when you get stuck, write in a notebook instead of on the computer, buy bags of air-popped popcorn because it doesn't make crumbs and your fingers won't get greasy. Restlessness is just part of the creative process, they've assured me, and time spent assessing the cheapest pastries in the café display case, down to the swirl of unmixed food coloring in the side of an orange spice muffin, isn't wasted. Or it *is* wasted, but in a necessary way, as Mary Ruefle would have it: "Wasted time cannot be filled, or changed into another habit; it is a necessary void of fomentation." Maira Kalman takes long walks. Alice Munro spends a lot of time looking out the window.

But because I was writing about boredom, this all seemed just a little too on the nose. My chosen topic was reflected in how I researched and wrote about said topic, or maybe it was the other way around: my daydream-filled and crumb-covered process had chosen the topic of boredom for me. Either way, it seemed imperative, even at such an early research stage, to get out of the library. I bought tickets to the WNYC event, which was part of the monthlong podcast project "Bored and Brilliant," and asked Joelle to come with me. The ticket price included a drink, so even if the hosts purposefully bored us (the website *did* promise "a semi-scientific experiment to test your creativity"), we would at least have the comfort of wine, no small thing in the cold heart of January.

More than a year later, I was reminded of that event in the confines of yet another library, NYU's Bobst. Unlike Columbia's stacks, clustered in the windowless core of a squat stone building that's nearly a century old, Bobst's are ringed around a twelve-story open atrium, with sunlight pouring in on all sides, every aisle and shelf as brightly lit as a beach vacation. Despite this, I don't find it very cheery, though I suspect this has less to do with the library itself and more to do with my introduction to it by Sonya, who went to NYU in the early aughts. Back when I started my job at a small college near NYU, which grants me access to Bobst's massive book reserves, she blurted out: "Ugh, I always hated that library," then added: "Sorry. It's just . . . there were a couple of suicides there my freshman year."

The suicides of strangers tend to stick with me, reminding me of people I've known who hurt themselves, or threatened to, or the automatic blip of fear I have when crossing bridges, a fundamental lack of trust in my own instincts for self-preservation. There was no way to escape the Bobst suicides after hearing about them, especially once I finally went to Bobst, on a hunt for nineteenth-century political cartoons requested by a research client. The Bobst suicides followed me into the lobby, up the elevator, into the stacks, and down the aisles of the art and architecture collection. They wouldn't let me be.

There's a saying, attributed to various historical figures: "The cure for boredom is curiosity. There is no cure for curiosity." But there *is*, at least in the Internet age; the easiest way to cure curiosity, in my experience, is to sate it—like Zorba in *Zorba the Greek*, who craved cherries constantly until he gorged himself on cherries, then never wanted them again. In a similar spirit, I left the stacks, found a library computer, and googled "Bobst suicide."

I don't know what I'd expected to find. Three people had died in the library, which was sad. Sadder still was that the circumstances weren't extraordinary—suicide is the second leading cause of death among college students, and jumping from a great height is one of the most common ways to go. It's a paradox of suicide, and death in general, that something so major and traumatic is also so commonplace. But one thing was different about the Bobst situation: in 2003, the year of two of the three suicides, a student began living in the library. For eight months, while these dramatic events unfolded on the floors above him, this real-life Stack Pirate slept across four chairs in the basement.

Steven Stanzak took up residence in the library because he was in financial straits (he washed himself in the library's public bathrooms and subsisted primarily on bagels and orange juice). But, as a writing student, he also knew that his situation held a certain amount of romance. He started a blog called *Homeless at NYU*, where he wrote that living in Bobst "seemed like something I could do, that would benefit me financially and creatively."

When occasional commenters accused him of being a phony, this is the line they tended to focus on, as if hunger for creativity couldn't possibly coexist with actual hunger. It's not uncommon to believe that such struggles are distinct; that people who haven't cleared the first two levels of Maslow's hierarchy of needs—sustenance and shelter—aren't capable of things higher up on the hierarchy, like love, confidence, and creativity. Though most modern psychologists disagree with this reading of the seventy-year-old hierarchy (if he were alive, Maslow himself might disagree, using his own argument that we are all "simultaneously worms and gods"), it's had remarkable staying power. I suppose it doesn't hurt that it reinforces capitalist ethics by making the poor seem sort of cavemanish, concerned with shelter and food but never with the state of their souls. In this warped view of reality, just *thinking* about art or philosophy is a privileged activity, reserved solely for the wealthy. In this spirit, creativity has become a commodity. Attendance at New York's Creativity Workshop, for example, will run you $895 for four days. If that seems steep, you could buy one of many long-titled books instead, such as *Creativity, Inc.: Overcoming the Unseen Forces That Stand in the Way of True Inspiration*; *Creative Confidence: Unleashing the Creative Potential Within Us All*; or *Big Magic: Creative Living Beyond Fear*, which is now also a podcast, free to listen to as long as you can afford a smartphone. Creativity is a coveted product, and Stanzak, who couldn't afford to pay rent, wanted it just as much as all the people, including me, who helped sell out WNYC's "Bored and Brilliant" event. Also like us, he'd sought it in a space that promised, in his words, "intense boredom."

Being bored by a place is one thing. Being bored by people—especially people you've paid to see, as we'd paid for the WNYC event—is another. Paying for boredom can make people angry, as evidenced by many reactions to *The Flick*, from red-faced muttering at intermission to complaint letters, citing length and banal dialogue. Sometimes, as with *The Flick*, boredom is a crucial part of the message, but how do you bore people without making them hate you?

"If something is boring after two minutes, try it for four," suggested John Cage. "If still boring, try it for eight, sixteen, thirty-two, and so on. Eventually one discovers that it is not boring at all but very interesting." His most famous example of this strategy is *4'33"*, a "performance" of total silence. He wanted his audience to appreciate silence like he did, to pay attention to the everyday noises—coughing, rustling, humming lightbulbs, hissing radiators—that we all usually tune out. It was a big ask, and one that didn't always pan out for Cage, who remains a controversial figure in music history. Cage's strategy seems to work better, or at least more consistently, for comedians such as Kristen Schaal and Kurt Braunohler, who have a stand-up bit in which they perform the same short song-and-dance routine over and over and over.

"After the third repetition, people laugh," Braunohler told the hosts of the podcast *Radiolab*. "But somewhere around the fourth time, it's really not funny. And then that changes to actual hatred. They're like, you stupid people, you two stupid people. But somewhere between like nine and eleven they're like, I *like* these stupid people."

There were no repetitive song-and-dance routines or performances of silence at the "Bored and Brilliant" event. Instead there was science. As a couple of hundred people crowded together, juggling plastic cups of wine and work bags and massive winter coats, our host, Manoush Zomorodi, explained that we'd be simulating an experiment conducted by the researchers Sandi Mann and Rebekah Cadman of the University of Central Lancashire. They'd split their study participants (all of whom were drafted from a local church) into three groups: one group read the phone book, one copied numbers from a phone book, and the last did whatever they pleased. Then everyone was asked to think of as many uses for a pair of plastic cups as possible; their answers were judged by both quantity and creativity.

Accordingly, Zomorodi split the audience into three groups: two-thirds of us got pages cut from phone books while the last third were given dispensation to hit the bar again. Joelle and I were in the reading group, and she dove in with gusto, tracing each line with her finger and pausing periodically to say things like, "Man, when was the last time I read a *phone book*?" or, "Whoa, I had no idea Manhattan had this many psychics!" Joelle, of everyone I know, is perhaps the most determined not to be bored.

Like the U.S. Postal Service's commitment to mail delivery, her pursuit of fun will not be hindered by snow or rain or heat or gloom of night. The effort she was putting into making the phone book fun was practically palpable.

I also hadn't read a phone book in a long time. But I was distracted by the thought that maybe Sandi Mann and I were related. There was a chance, though not a large one. We're not as ubiquitous as Smiths or Joneses, but there are a lot of Manns out there. There are even a lot of Mary Manns, though it seems that most of them are long-deceased wives of nineteenth-century preachers. The first time I googled my name, in order to find the link to an essay, I ended up studying image after image of stern black-and-white women. We Mary Manns are a dull lot. I remember initially finding this comforting, then worrying about that reaction. What did it mean to find comfort in the faces of women who looked as if they'd all eaten the same breakfast every day for their whole lives (probably oatmeal) and *liked it*?

"Okay!" called Zomorodi from the front of the room. "We're passing around Post-its and a few small items. Please take the next five minutes to write down any use you can think of for the items you receive."

I hadn't got beyond the first couple of lines of my phone book pages, but that turned out to be the point. Those who copied down the phone book numbers had to focus to complete the task and could daydream only if they paused in their work, like the IRS employee in David Foster Wallace's paean to boredom, *The Pale King*, who "did two more returns, then another one, then flexed his buttocks and held to a count of ten and imagined a warm pretty beach with mellow surf, as instructed in orientation the previous month. Then he did two more returns . . ." Those of us who just read the phone book, on the other hand, could allow our minds to relax and daydream willy-nilly, which was good, at least according to Sandi Mann, because "it is daydreaming that leads to an increase in creativity."

We were expected to have the most creative uses for our items, which turned out to be sponges and plastic utensils. The people who copied down phone numbers would be less creative, but would still have more answers than the group at the bar, whose laughter and conversation had increased in volume over the course of the exercise, giving the event space the feel of an office party in the early stages: some employees popping champagne while others scramble to finish work. They were the least creative people in the room, in theory, but it sounded like they were having way more fun.

Well, of course, Matthew Killingsworth might say—most of them are probably happier. In 2010, Killingsworth, then a researcher at Harvard, introduced an app to track people's happiness. He ended up with data from more than fifteen thousand people, from ages eighteen to eighty-eight and from all over the world, and found that, across the board, we're substantially *less* happy when daydreaming. "Mind-wandering," he reported in a TED talk the following year, "very likely seems to be an actual cause, and not merely a consequence, of unhappiness."

The simple key to happiness would seem to be: don't let your mind wander. But then you lose that creative fuel that Sandi Mann says daydreaming gives us. And anyway, we don't have that much choice. Killingsworth's research found that, while some activities cause our minds to wander more than others, everybody daydreams at least 30 percent of the time, during *all activities* except sex (when we daydream only 10 percent of the time). Even the people laughing at the bar weren't all "in the moment," every moment. As they returned to their seats to join the rest of us in scribbling down ideas, sipping drinks and checking phones, I looked around and tried to guess which itinerant minds were floating away from their bodies, daydreaming about sex with someone they'd met at the bar, revisiting their pasts or envisioning their futures; our bodies were all in the room, but our minds might be anywhere, wandering down the street to an office building or across the country to Los Angeles or over the ocean to the Republic of Georgia or off to another galaxy altogether.

Back in the library, I wasn't just daydreaming, I was daydreaming *about daydreaming*, jolted back to the present only by the clatter of wheels as a janitor rolled a trashcan past the computer station. The ebb and flow of library life was, had been, always is, happening all around me: janitors and librarians and security guards performing daily routines; students turning pages and sipping contraband coffee and whispering with each other and taking notes, pens scratching on paper. Maybe one of them was scheming to be the next Stack Pirate. Certainly many of them were also daydreaming. You're never alone in daydreaming, especially in the library. Even the books whisper of daydreaming minds, those of the authors and of their characters: Don Quixote's delusions, Mrs. Dalloway's nostalgia, Walter Mitty's wholly fictional escapades. "The act of writing both draws on and generates imaginative vitality," writes the scholar Patricia Meyer Spacks, herself the author of a literary history of boredom. "So does the act of reading."

From movies, we have some idea what the writer in this scenario looks like: Nicole Kidman as Virginia Woolf, muttering to herself in front of her momentarily forgotten nieces and nephews in *The Hours*, or Nicolas Cage as Charlie Kaufman, pacing and ranting into a tape recorder in *Adaptation*. We've seen plenty of writer representations, written (of course) by writers, and we know more about the writer every year. The writer now has a blog, a Twitter profile, and a Facebook page; writers script the shows that stream on Netflix, use of which accounts for more than a third of all U.S. Internet traffic, as well as many of the four hundred hours of video uploaded to YouTube every single minute. The writer makes so many things, of such variety, that the businessman has taken to calling it all content, just to make it easier to talk about. We are content creators, and we are legion—nobody could read and watch all the things being written at this exact moment even if they dedicated their whole lives to the task. Who is this great quantity of stuff *for*?

It's a question that might preoccupy anyone who makes stuff, not just writers. Sonya loved working at a small start-up because she got to play a vital part in the growth of a company. A detective solves crimes to protect people; a soldier defends people. One of my students, getting her degree in visual art, has written a quote by the poet Aracelis Girmay across her notebook: "Who or what does this work care for?" To have a purpose is to be useful, and that means not just making stuff, but making stuff specifically for others, as in that Japanese legend about two friends, one who played the harp and one who listened. When the listening friend died, the harpist "cut the strings of his harp and never played again."

What I've always liked best about this story is how the friends are described, "one who played the harp skillfully and one who listened skillfully." The listener's skill is just as useful as that of the musician, the act of listening just as imbued with purpose as the act of making music. For either of them to have purpose, the other has to exist.

Skillful listening, in this context, is like a type of creativity all its own, the ability to catch a concept or feeling and bring it to life; while the harpist plays a song about mountains, the friend "can see the mountains before us." In *H Is for Hawk*, Helen Macdonald describes her home briefly—one paragraph—and as I read it I knew everything about the place, from the floor plan to where she keeps the spoons, scads of details she hadn't offered. Good writing begets good reading, and good reading fills the mind with whole worlds to visit, free of charge, places to go when you're bored or lonely or lying in bed unable to sleep.

A large-scale example of this relationship is the Cuban tradition of the tobacco reader. Rolling cigars is tedious work that requires concentration, like copying phone numbers or checking tax returns. It's hard to daydream while doing this kind of work, but easy to listen to someone else's daydreams, and that's where the tobacco reader comes in, paid to read aloud on the factory floor.

While the authors aren't actually with the cigar rollers, they are at common purposes, since, as Spacks notes, "the need to refute boredom's deadening power impels the writer's productivity and the reader's engagement." For well over a hundred years, tobacco readers—and the authors whose work they read—have rescued cigar rollers from boredom, helping them build whole universes of worlds in their minds. The employees, in turn, have expanded literary lore by suggesting that cigar brands be named after characters in their favorite stories, resulting in the Romeo y Julieta and the legendary Montecristo.

Inspired by the tobacco reader tradition, the writer Valeria Luiselli began collaborating with Mexico City's Jumex juice factory workers in 2013. She'd send a new piece of writing to the factory each week, which the workers would read and discuss, sending her their thoughts afterward. The writer's daydreams enriched the factory workers' experience, and vice versa; their discussions provided personal anecdotes and "directed the course of the narrative" for the resultant book: *The Story of My Teeth* is about the hopes, dreams, and delusions of a factory guard turned auctioneer; the whispered daydreams of Jumex factory workers joining those of Woolf and Cervantes, Shakespeare and Alexandre Dumas, on the library shelves.

WNYC's "Bored and Brilliant" experiment didn't go exactly to plan. We all turned in our Post-its, but it wasn't clear which group had ended up with more creative uses for sponges and utensils, and Zomorodi reminded us that the experiment was only "semi-scientific." There was an understanding that we were all distracted by the nature of the event—there's this feeling in the air, sometimes, at sold-out New York events, a communal rush of being *the ones who made it*, heightened in this case by free drinks and an especially unique activity. Boredom in 2015 was becoming something of a hot topic, an old feeling made new by media attention, and here we were at the very cusp of the trend. Everyone was sort of flushed and manic. Joelle had written out idea after idea, so many that she had to request more Post-its, muttering: "What about flags? Yeah, little flags. Or wait, earrings!" I was impressed, but too distracted to emulate her, lost this time not in daydreaming but in eavesdropping.

"I just think that technology keeps us too *in it*, you know?" a woman to the left and slightly behind us was saying to the man next to her. "My team, they're *always* online, and I can point to where every one of their ideas comes from. It's like, guys, take a walk! *Think!* Don't just give me recycled campaigns from Toms or whatever. Those shoes are ugly anyway."

"Right, right, right." The guy sounded like he'd just chugged a Red Bull. "But also, wrong. Because there are no new ideas, you know what I'm saying? The thing is creative stealing, right, it's the retro appeal, it's putting Coke back into glass bottles. You don't want to be New Coke, do you, Gina? I don't think you want to be New Coke."

"Christ," groaned the woman, presumably Gina. "Is that really my choice, glass bottle or New Coke? I hate this job. I swear, some days I would sell my soul for a brand-new idea."

The guy laughed, an outsized guffaw. "Christ," he sputtered. "Welcome to marketing, Gina."

Right, I thought, absently doodling on my Post-it, *marketers*. For every artist or writer hoping for a flash of creative inspiration, there are a thousand marketers depending on one for their company's success, not to mention their own. With so many new products appearing all the time, marketing is more vital, and more difficult, than it's ever been before. My marketing friend Erica calls it "a war for your mind." There is tremendous pressure to make everything seem new and interesting, or watch it fail. "An age of constant invention," reads a *New York Times* article about tech start-ups that flop, "naturally begets one of constant failure."

Stressful, I wrote in looping cursive, near a (poor) sketch of the guest lecturers. There were two of them sitting up onstage, one the author of a popular blog and the other a visual artist, both diligently filling out Post-its. Before the boredom experiment, the artist had shown us photos she'd taken on airplanes of things she'd made—including costumes she constructed and wore in the lavatory—using only stuff she found on said airplanes: peanuts, napkins, in-flight magazines, toilet seat covers, all of it documented only with her cell phone. She called the series *Seat Assignment*. She was funny, a descriptor that's often used synonymously with "not boring." I thought I'd note down her name, maybe look her up later, see if she'd be willing to talk with me about how she's been able to address boredom in her work while remaining not boring. *Nina Katchadourian*, I wrote under the highly inaccurate sketch, and when the event aides came around to collect our Post-its, I had nothing to give them.

Nina, as it turns out, teaches at NYU, her office building just down the street from Bobst. We met in the lobby and went up to her office in the elevator together. She's very small, and next to her I felt messy and cumbersome. This probably also had something to do with her being the first fellow boredom investigator I'd been able to meet in person. There'd been plenty of Skypes and calls and e-mails, but the boredom community is small and far-flung. There *is* a yearly boredom conference where they all gather, but it's in Poland, and getting there is criminally expensive. Still, I spent a long time lusting after that conference. There was no place to register online if you weren't presenting a paper, so I e-mailed to ask if it was possible to attend as an observer and how much that would cost. A man named Mariusz wrote back, confused as to exactly what I wanted, and we had a brief back-and-forth where I felt the need to explain that I live in New York, where many events end up selling out. "We simply haven't expected such a possibility," he explained. "The conference is completely open for the public." Unfortunately this didn't change the fact that I didn't have the money to fly to Poland. Which was just as well, I reasoned as a way to console myself, since I wanted to learn about boredom, not jet-setting.

Nina's *Seat Assignment* is about both. She has to fly a lot for work anyway, she explained once we were sitting in her office, and she's a restless, easily distractible person by nature. "I thought it would be interesting to contemplate a project that would allow me to work with my own worst tendencies," she told me, and I felt my cheeks warm with the pleasant and disorienting embarrassment of having immediate affinity for someone.

Airplanes have long been fecund places for Nina, just like trains are for Baratunde. Before *Seat Assignment*, just for fun, she made a music video about all the cats in *SkyMall* magazine. The result, "*SkyMall* Kitties," ended up going viral. "SkyMall *kitties / kitties everywhere /* SkyMall *kitties / kitties of the aaaair . . .*"

"*SkyMall* Kitties" lives on YouTube, and is maybe her most Internet-y work, slotting in nicely with other people's boredom creations that find their home online: photographs of pictures shoveled into the snow by a bored Russian janitor, radar images of penises and airplanes drawn by the flight paths of bored pilots, J. D. Witherspoon's hypercatchy "I'm Bored" rap video. Despite being made by adults, these creations seem to belong to the Internet content category that the *New York Times* tech writer Jenna Wortham calls borecore, "the never-to-be-viral output that comes from mixing powerful devices and a lifetime of social-media training with regular, old teenage boredom."

Nina does spend a lot of time online, and though sometimes she gets ideas while zigzagging around the Internet, she's not thrilled about how much time she spends on what she calls "the most mundane distractions": Facebook, e-mail, news sites. "Fuck the Internet," she said, laughing, as our phones took turns buzzing on the desk between us. "It's so useful and so terrible! I have to go to the library more. There's the same opportunity for free association, but it's only about books, it's not *also* about your correspondence, your social media . . ."

"Fewer land mines," I suggested, thinking of my own inbox, which I check all the time even though I know already that it's bulging with tasks from multiple jobs, paperless bills to pay, wedding save-the-dates, forwarded articles about boredom from friends, and guilt-inducing fund-raising e-mails from various organizations. (Including the public library, which I frequent because I'm broke. Still, I give them money when I can, strong-armed by stories of foster kids learning to read. The library knows a mark when they meet one.)

"Exactly," Nina concurred. "I was walking down the street yesterday, phone in pocket, my arms full of things I'd just picked up from my framer, and it was an interesting moment because it was only a couple minutes before I wanted my phone and I realized: I'm carrying things, I can't reach for the phone. I have to just walk and look and think, walk and look and think. I really do want more of that time in my day-to-day."

Baratunde, by far the most Internet-y person that I know, told me the same thing: "I want to build more unstimulated time into my day." We'd talked about how this has become a clichéd desire—everyone wants it, nobody knows quite how to get it, so we just keep talking about it, over and over, like we do about happiness, or creativity. For Nina, though, it's especially vital because her work is built around "the pretty basic act of paying attention to things that are generally overlooked."

"There are a lot of things we don't notice, or don't spend enough time with, that become interesting if you spend time with them," she said, adding: "This is the sort of thing a lot of artists might say these days. There's a lot of art that comes from this place." We talked then about art that celebrates the mundane, the overlooked, and the repetitive. I see this kind of art everywhere, now that I'm looking for it, though it's probably been around me all along. There are even projects that address boredom directly, such as Nargess Hashemi's *The Pleasure in Boredom*, a series of intricate sketches that resemble rugs and reference the "monotonous repetition, constraint and order of domestic life, and the restrictions in modern Tehran, especially for women."

According to Hashemi, *The Pleasure in Boredom* was inspired by an essay—"Pleasures of Boredom"—by the art critic Ernst Gombrich that is about doodling and which I ended up reading in Bobst on that same windy day—many months after interviewing Nina; the day I learned about student suicides and Steven Stanzak the Stack Pirate and how much I hadn't known about that one building, how little I probably know still. *There are a lot of things we don't notice.* There are a lot of ordinary things, like Bobst, like boredom, that only need a bit of research to become extraordinary.

Gombrich, similarly, was inspired by the discovery of doodles in the eighteenth-century ledgers of the Banco di Napoli to begin a research project, searching for other doodles and doodlers through the ages, from sketches in Leonardo da Vinci's fifteenth-century journals to drawings in the margins of Dostoyevsky's nineteenth-century manuscripts. "It is hard, if not wholly impossible, to concentrate for any length of time on a monotonous task," wrote Gombrich. "Try as we may, our mind begins to wander and sooner or later the quality of the work will suffer." But Gombrich suggested this isn't something we need to worry too much about because we've developed release valves for ourselves, habits and behaviors that prevent boredom from building up during monotonous work and having a negative effect on both the person doing the work and the final product. "This danger is diminished," he wrote, "by keeping the mind mildly occupied in another way during the performance of an almost mechanical task." Like cigar factory employees in Cuba, both Rubens and Mozart liked to be read to while they worked. Others—bankers and artists and me, at the WNYC event—like to doodle. Nina likes to sew and whittle ("My hands are busy and my head is free in a really interesting way)."

I couldn't help, then, but look at her hands: they were still, wrapped around one of her knees as she leaned back in her chair, thinking, presumably, about whittling and daydreaming.

But there's more to boredom than that. I knew it; we both knew it. I wanted to get there but wasn't sure how, so I began to tell her about all the people I'd spoken with about boredom: my cousin Connie in the orange juice cannery, Sonya watching the clock in a corporate office, soldiers watching porn in Iraq, and Eastwood and Danckert studying boredom and depression in a lab. "Oh, Eastwood! I've read him," Nina said. "There's another researcher, Smallwood, and I used to mix them up."

"Smallwood!" I felt the rush of one stamp collector meeting another, in an era when hardly anybody even sends mail anymore. "Yeah, I know him—the daydreaming guy. So, you know, all these people research different parts of boredom, or experience it in different ways. There's so much to it besides creativity. Like, anxious boredom, or irritable—"

"Or depressive," she cut in. "There have been days sometimes, to be really honest, where I think, *How can I be so busy and still feel a little bit bored?* When you're starting to feel frustrated and exhausted by your own project, and it's become uninteresting to you, there's that sort of terrible boredom. Like, 'I don't even *like* my work right now!'" With the word "like," she slammed her hand down on her desk. She was no longer leaning back in her chair.

Her office windows looked out onto the hallway and it was hard to tell how long we'd been speaking, holding our boredom conference of two. The shelves on the wall behind her were filled with books. Her dad wrote a book about guilt, she told me, and for ten years he'd taught a college course on the difference between guilt and shame. We have something else in common besides boredom, I told her—my dad is a priest. I'm familiar with guilt. That was one of the reasons for my initial interest in boredom, I explained, because I'd always attached so much guilt to it, feeling the old and widespread shame that stems from its roots as the monk's vice, acedia.

Nina began to talk about her dad, and then stopped. "First," she said, "you need to know that my brother is a professional windsurfer." He's a very good one, she explained, very dedicated and single-minded about the sport, able to fall into flow easily once he steps onto his board, and at one point Nina decided to do a radio program about his relationship with wind, and her family's relationship to his relationship with wind. "My dad," she said, "he told me, 'There are lots of things in my life that I've been interested in, and things that I care about, but I've never had a passion. Your brother has a passion.'"

As she spoke her eyes wandered the shelves, the books and papers, the window's view of the administrative hallway, dingily carpeted and poorly lit, as such hallways always tend to be. I thought about my own parents. Did they have passions? I thought about their jobs. My dad loves God, but seems to find working for him more draining than anything else. My mom has always just tolerated being a nurse. She's been talking about other jobs she might do for as long as I can remember. When I was small and we lived close to my grandparents, she kept art supplies in my grandmother's attic, and when we were visiting overnight she would occasionally go upstairs, sit in front of the window, and paint watercolors, beach scenes mostly. She's recently picked painting back up again, and she sent me a beach scene in the mail the other day, looking just how I remembered them: blue horizon line, curve of beach, spikes of sea grass in both bottom corners, and the backlit silhouettes of a couple of seagulls coming in from the left. Maybe these paintings were her passion. Or maybe her passion was the people she made the paintings for, a thought that plucked a string inside me, a minor chord. Several parents had told me how guilty they felt for being bored while hanging out with their kids, the worry they had that their love was flawed; for grown kids, for me at least, there's guilt in failing to appreciate being loved. *Call Mom*, I wrote in the notebook on my lap.

Out loud I said: "I'm not so sure I know what it means to have a passion. It's more complicated than I used to think."

Nina nodded. "I think it's something like the opposite of boredom," she said. "I guess it's not an accident that there is a sort of religious flavor to both words. With passion you're sort of . . . utterly devoted to something, in a way where you haven't even had a choice; it's just overtaken you."

"Is that what art is like for you?"

"No." She winced. "I would not say that, actually. I would not say that about myself." She reminded me, then, of what she'd said about going through bored stretches, which are not the norm for her, but do come regularly enough, even when she has a lot of projects going. "I think, for artists, writers, and musicians, the fantasy is that those people are never bored, and the work is never boring, because it's this pinnacle of passionate engagement. So you feel like you're not just letting yourself down if you're bored, you're letting down the whole aura of the thing. It makes me feel ungrateful. Like an ungrateful wretch."

And that's really the "sin" of boredom, at least the way our culture tends to see it: boredom is the failure to appreciate, a sin against love and art and nature. But knowing that doesn't make it go away. It just makes you feel shittier, bored *and* ungrateful. "Yeah," I said. "I know what you mean."

We stewed in guilt together for a moment. She looked at her bookshelf. I looked over the questions I'd wanted to ask, running over in my head what other artists and writers have said about what Nina had described. There were many, from F. Scott Fitzgerald to Adele, but my favorite is by Alice Dunbar-Nelson, widow of Paul Laurence Dunbar and a poet in her own right, but female and black and thus doubly overlooked, lacking possibilities not because she was trapped geographically, like the Georgians, but because she was trapped in a body and in an era that shamed that body. "Bored!" she'd written in her diary. "I don't think I have ever been so completely bored in all my life. Wrote Bobbo I was afraid I'd get into mischief. Bored to tears. Or is it biliousness? Still I'm bored! Tired of doing nothing, of being nobody, of being shunted to the shelf. But I have nothing. Fay says if you have an idea, it will be heard. My mind is a blank. Ye gods! Must I always be at the lower middle of the ladder?"

Nelson was bored, resentful, and most of all stuck. This inertia lingered until a few days later, when, around three in the afternoon, "words leapt at me from somewhere and I began and finished 'Harlem John Henry Views the Airmada,' a poem in blank verse, with spirituals running through. A weird thing, five pages long, which left me in two hours' time as limp as a rag." Sometimes that just happens, ideas need to percolate, to irritate, to hover around the edges, taunting and teasing, refusing to arrive until they're good and ready; "your poems," in the words of Mary Ruefle, "speak out of your wasted time," and there's nothing we can do to make them speak sooner. We just have to let our limited time be wasted, wait it out, and try to feel as okay about that as possible. It helps if this wasted time is built into the structure of your job, like in moviemaking. "You might do forty takes of the same scene," the actress Greta Lee told me. "It's mind-numbingly boring, but there's something to wearing out your body and mind over hours that really ends up working in everyone's favor. You do less. You get out of your own way."

Back in her office, Nina turned toward me and pulled her tiny frame erect. "Art is work," she said decisively. "And work is boring sometimes. I get in the middle of projects where I think, 'Why did I think I wanted to do

this? I don't want to do this!' But then, more often than
not, there's a rewarding moment at the end where the
thing is done and I'm *really* glad I didn't give it up."

Months later. A different season, the same street. I exited
Bobst, stepping out into the fresh rain-flecked gusts of
March in Manhattan. I wasn't done with the library—I'd be
back later that week—but I was done for the day. I walked
through Washington Square Park, paths and manicured
lawns and flowerbeds covering over what used to be a
burial ground. Dogs yapped and scrapped in the dog run
and teens skateboarded and a guy was playing a piano on
wheels while another man danced alone in the grass. At
the West Fourth Street station I got on the B train uptown.
I was meeting Rachel at the planetarium, and on the way,
as usual, I took notes: woman, sixties, *Candy Crush*; man,
thirties, staring at grocery delivery service ad with glazed
eyes, possibly sleeping with eyes open; man, twenties, Facebook; woman, forties to fifties, glaring into middle distance, grinds teeth whenever train slows; boy, maybe five,
asking his weary-eyed mom question after question. I'd
need a new notebook soon; this one was nearly full. That's
the thing about studying something so pervasive. Who
needs to go to Poland for a boredom conference when
you have subway cars full of people giving free demon-
strations every day of the week?

The planetarium was nearly full by the time I got there
and found Rachel, saving a seat for me in the blue pre-
show light. The show, a lecture on "the architecture of

the universe," was starting soon in the round room beneath the planetarium's dome. They never use the dome enough at these lectures, in my opinion, but it's worth it even for the little bit that they do, especially when they use the live-feed feature, zooming around the galaxy from one actively burning star to another. Exploring space, even remotely like this, makes me feel incredibly small, maybe something akin to what Ernest Becker calls the "feeling of inferiority in the face of the massive transcendence of creation," but also exhilarated, unshackled for the moment from daily concerns about how I spend my time and what it's all for, my fears switched off while my eyes are trained on bigger things.

The lecture was probably interesting, but definitely over my head. Polygons and low-density mass, computer models of the universe and graphs of its expansion. My mind wandered. *It's good for creativity*, I reminded myself. And *your poems speak out of your wasted time*. Which means it isn't wasted at all. There are infinite universes, said the lecturer, expanding infinitely. Time washed over me, around me, and it was fine if some of it was wasted. It was such a relief that it was fine. Stephen Hawking was bored in school; I'd read that somewhere. So was Einstein. It was actually Einstein's birthday. I know because the lecturer told us so when he brought up Einstein's cosmological constant. It's -1, which means as much to me as 42 being the answer to life, the universe, and everything.

A gentle industrial roar rose around us. "Don't be alarmed," said the lecturer, pausing in his lecture. "They're just warming up the projectors." The blue lights dimmed and went out. For a moment the room was pitch-black. Infinite bubble universes, the lecturer went on, float in an infinitely expanding inflationary sea. The model he'd showed looked nothing like any sea; it looked like a human brain, or maybe a sea sponge. Rachel yawned. The guy on my other side yawned. I yawned. And then the light changed, and above us, all around us, was the universe.

EPILOGUE

The more I heard people deride or deny it, the more I wanted to know about boredom, like how getting lunch detention for flipping the bird in second grade (which I only did because Adam Z did it first, and he only did it because his older brother had done it the night before) ended up making me more curious than repentant. The teacher's response was so dramatic and swift for such an innocuous gesture. It was a finger. Wherein lay its power? The responses when I said the words "bored" and "boring" were similarly perplexing. Whether it was annoyance or relief, the words always triggered something emotional.

For this reason, I never used to talk about boredom. I tried not to even think about it. There were always other, more pressing issues, such as rent and relationships. It was only once I made the decision to read and learn about boredom, and especially once I began talking to other people about it, that I realized how large a role it played in my own life. Maybe every book topic is like that, and if I'd spent all this time researching spaghetti I'd feel intimately and powerfully connected to spaghetti instead. But my relationship with boredom was something different from a connection. The things I learned about boredom, and the ways I learned to talk about it, actually proved useful. I began to pay more attention to what bores me and why, which helped me work better, communicate better, and make better choices. The tribulations of my students were also easier to understand and sympathize with, as I watched them grow restless with certain topics or projects or become paralyzed over bigger decisions, such as choosing career paths or life partners. Learning about boredom helped me understand the limitations of patience and accept the occasional failures of love. Many things that were once frightening—commitment, for example—are slightly less so now.

Not that it's all been happy revelation after revelation. As documented in the preceding chapters, I ended up finding things in myself that I'd rather weren't there: easy irritability, loneliness that I carry with me into crowds, and a tendency toward depression that's always been in my family but which I never wanted to acknowledge in myself. I also had to spend an excessive amount of time with a few uncomfortable topics, such as infidelity and death, and the fact that I was thinking about these things so much made me a very weird person to be around sometimes. But this was always going to be part of the project; I knew going into it that boredom is universally uncomfortable, and that the feelings and causes surrounding it probably would be too.

What I didn't know going into the project, but I quickly learned, was that researching boredom meant researching everything. Like other moods—happiness, sadness, anger—it pops up in every facet of existence, from work to love to war. In the process of researching this book I got to speak with scientists and soldiers, artists and laborers. I got to spend my days reading the words of prisoners and priests and revisiting favorite old books by authors I wish I could have had the chance to interview, such as Miguel de Cervantes, Agatha Christie, and James Baldwin. I'm extraordinarily grateful for all these people, the deceased and the living. There isn't really a "cure" for boredom—and if there were, I'm not sure I'd want it— but if there's anything that alleviates the itchy, everyday restlessness of this troublesome mood, it's other people.

SELECTED BIBLIOGRAPHY

Ansari, Aziz, and Eric Klinenberg. *Modern Romance*. New York: Penguin Press, 2015.

Becker, Ernest. *The Denial of Death*. New York: Free Press, 1997.

Blake, William. "Voices from Solitary: A Sentence Worse Than Death." SolitaryWatch.com, March 11, 2013.

Boianjiu, Shani. *The People of Forever Are Not Afraid*. New York: Hogarth, 2012.

Brendon, Piers. *Thomas Cook: 150 Years of Popular Tourism*. London: Secker & Warburg, 1991.

Cage, John. *Silence: Lectures and Writings*. Middletown, CT: Wesleyan University Press, 1961.

Cervantes, Miguel de. *Don Quixote*. Translated by Edith Grossman. New York: Ecco, 2003.

Chaucer, Geoffrey. *The Canterbury Tales*. Translated into Modern English by Nevill Coghill. London and New York: Penguin Books, 2003.

Cohen, Erik. *Contemporary Tourism: Diversity and Change*. Amsterdam: Elsevier, 2004.

Csikszentmihalyi, Mihaly. *Flow: The Psychology of Optimal Experience*. New York: Harper & Row, 1990.

Dann, Graham. *The Language of Tourism: A Sociolinguistic Perspective*. Wallingford, UK: CAB International, 1996.

Dunbar-Nelson, Alice. *Give Us Each Day: The Diary of Alice Dunbar-Nelson*. Edited by Gloria T. Hull. New York: W. W. Norton, 1984.

Frederiksen, Martin Demant. *Young Men, Time, and Boredom in the Republic of Georgia*. Philadelphia: Temple University Press, 2013.

Fromm, Erich. *The Anatomy of Human Destructiveness*. New York: Holt, Rinehart and Winston, 1973.

Fussell, Paul. *Wartime: Understanding and Behavior in the Second World War*. New York: Oxford University Press, 1989.

Gana, Kamel, Raphael Trouillet, Bettina Martin, and Leatitia Toffart. "The Relationship Between Boredom Proneness and Solitary Sexual Behaviors in Adults." *Social Behavior and Personality* 29, no. 4 (June 2001): 385–90.

Goldberg, Yael K., John D. Eastwood, Jennifer LaGuardia, and James Danckert. "Boredom: An Emotional Experience Distinct from Apathy, Anhedonia, or Depression." *Journal of Social and Clinical Psychology* 30, no. 6 (June 2011): 647–66.

Gombrich, E. H. *The Uses of Images: Studies in the Social Function of Art and Visual Communication*. London: Phaidon, 1999.

Hamper, Ben. *Rivethead: Tales from the Assembly Line*. New York: Warner Books, 1991.

Hardaker, Claire. "Uh. . . . Not to Be Nitpicky,,,,,but . . . the Past Tense of Drag Is Dragged, not Drug: An Overview of Trolling Strategies." *Journal of Language Aggression and Conflict* 1, no. 1 (June 2013): 58–86.

Healy, Seán Desmond. *Boredom, Self, and Culture*. Rutherford, NJ: Fairleigh Dickinson University Press, 1984.

Kelly, John C. "Work: Or Boredom?" *The Irish Monthly* 77, no. 916 (1949): 443–47.

Killingsworth, Matthew A., and Daniel T. Gilbert. "A Wandering Mind Is an Unhappy Mind." *Science* 330, no. 6006 (November 2010): 932.

Kincaid, Jamaica. *A Small Place*. New York: Farrar, Straus and Giroux, 1988.

Lawrence, D. H. *Phoenix: The Posthumous Papers of D. H. Lawrence*. Edited by Edward D. McDonald. New York: Viking, 1936.

Luiselli, Valeria. *The Story of My Teeth*. Translated by Christina MacSweeney. Minneapolis: Coffee House Press, 2015.

Lutz, Tom. *Doing Nothing: A History of Loafers, Loungers, Slackers, and Bums in America*. New York: Farrar, Straus and Giroux, 2006.

McLeod, Lisa Earle. *Selling with Noble Purpose: How to Drive Revenue and Do Work That Makes You Proud*. Hoboken, NJ: John Wiley & Sons, 2012.

Melville, Herman. *Moby-Dick; or, The Whale*. New York: Barnes & Noble Books, 1994.

Murray, Paul. *Skippy Dies*. New York: Faber & Faber, 2010.

Norris, Kathleen. *Acedia & Me: A Marriage, Monks, and a Writer's Life*. New York: Riverhead Books, 2008.

Perel, Esther. *Mating in Captivity: Unlocking Erotic Intelligence*. New York: Harper, 2006.

Phillips, Adam. *On Kissing, Tickling, and Being Bored: Psychoanalytic Essays on the Unexamined Life*. Cambridge, MA: Harvard University Press, 1993.

Postman, Neil. *Amusing Ourselves to Death: Public Discourse in the Age of Show Business*. New York: Viking, 1985.

Raposa, Michael L. *Boredom and the Religious Imagination*. Charlottesville: University Press of Virginia, 1999.

Ruefle, Mary. *Madness, Rack, and Honey: Collected Lectures*. Seattle: Wave Books, 2012.

———. "Milk Shake." *The Paris Review*, Spring 2016.

Russell, Bertrand. *Conquest of Happiness*. New York: W. W. Norton, 1971.

Solomon, Andrew. *The Noonday Demon: An Atlas of Depression*. New York: Scribner, 2001.

Spacks, Patricia Meyer. *Boredom: The Literary History of a State of Mind*. Chicago: University of Chicago Press, 1995.

Swofford, Anthony. *Jarhead: A Marine's Chronicle of the Gulf War and Other Battles*. New York: Scribner, 2003.

Terkel, Studs. *Working: People Talk About What They Do All Day and How They Feel About What They Do*. New York: New Press, 1972.

Tilburg, Wijnand A. P. van, and Eric R. Igou. "On Boredom: Lack of Challenge and Meaning as Distinct Boredom Experiences." *Motivation and Emotion* 36, no. 2 (June 2012): 181–94.

Tunariu, Aneta D., and Paula Reavey. "Men in Love: Living with Sexual Boredom." *Sexual and Relationship Therapy* 18, no. 1 (February 2003): 63–94.

Turner, Brian. *My Life as a Foreign Country*. New York: W. W. Norton, 2014.

Vowell, Sarah. *Lafayette in the Somewhat United States*. New York: Riverhead Books, 2015.

Wallace, David Foster. *The Pale King: An Unfinished Novel*. New York: Little, Brown, 2011.

Watt, John D., and Jackie E. Ewing. "Toward the Development and Validation of a Measure of Sexual Boredom." *Journal of Sex Research* 33, no. 1 (1996): 57–66.

ACKNOWLEDGMENTS

My thanks go first to the people who made this book possible: my wonderful and sympathetic agent, Monika Verma, and superb editors, Emily Bell and Maya Binyam.

For being so generous with their time and thoughts, many thanks and probably a few drinks are owed to Nate Harris, Erica Rosen, Brian Turner, Ruti Wajnberg, Lindsay Johnson, Leslie Abitz, Ashley Ford, Duane Bond, Baratunde Thurston, Nina Katchadourian, Connie Hart, Rani Mackevich, Ken Tomlinson, Blythe Jones, Teresa Cheng, Megan Johnson, Andrew Solomon, Martin Demant Frederiksen, Elisabeth Prammer, Wijnand van Tilburg, James Danckert, Deborah Anapol, Walker Muncy, Ashley Patrick, Teresa Belton, Javier Perez-Albert, John Eastwood, Dior Vargas, Gracie Landes, Jeff Kling, Erik Ringmar, Jorg Kustermans, Randi Gunther, Susan Wright, Sylvia Rosenfeld, and Greta Lee. For the time and space to work, many thanks also to the Catwalk Institute.

For showing me what it is to be both a hardworking writer and a good person, I couldn't have asked for better models than

Patty O'Toole, Stacy Schiff, Megan Hustad, Sheila Heti, Leanne Shapton, and Heidi Julavits.

And for everything else—walks, talks, reading, snack tours, and bad jokes—I'd like to thank Denise and Fred Mann, Madeline Catanzarite, Grant Jones, Rachel Nackman, Martha Guenther, Mattea Kramer, Kate Stevens, Allison Beatrice, Ariel Hubbard, Joelle Asaro-Berman, and Maya Jonesmann. What would I be without you? Dumber, I suspect. And quite a bit more boring.